OUT OF WORK
NOT
OUT OF WORTH

OUT OF WORK
NOT
OUT OF WORTH

Navigating the Emotional Side of Job Loss

David Petrovay, PhD

Out of Work... Not Out of Worth
Navigating The Emotional Side Of Job Loss
2nd Edition

david@davidpetrovaycoaching.com
www.davidpetrovaycoaching.com

ISBN: (paperback) 979-8-9901583-0-6

Printed in the United States of America

What readers are saying...

This is essential reading for those dark days of doubt and frustration... David is a ray of sunshine. Yes, you have to do the work, but he holds you up with sensitivity and encouragement in every word.

What I enjoyed the most about the book is that the author took the time to create exercises allowing me to see areas in my life where things were missing. The questions had me reflecting on where I was, where I am, and what motivates me in my job. I learned so much about myself, my co-workers, and managers using the exercises provided.

I've completed a graduate level course on career counseling and I found Dr. Petrovay's book to cover key concepts in a far more positive and helpful way than the graduate course I completed. The reflective exercises are important tools that can help an individual become reacquainted with areas of strength and interest, while also considering new opportunities that are a good fit.

You feel like you are listening to a close friend when you read this book. If you have ever felt like no one understands, read the book and you won't feel disappointed. You will be amazed at how you feel when you finish this book.

This book engages the reader to explore the power of transition, as the space between jobs is really a transition from one to another. Transitions make up most of our life, yet we rarely harness that transition time to our benefit. David Petrovay shows us the way in a well-written and motivational book.

Dr. Petrovay's book begins with a revealing and relevant review of his own career trajectory, which clearly indicates both his competence, intention, and suitability to write such a book as he did. Then, he introduces core concepts the person looking to transition careers should absolutely embody: self-confidence, perseverance, acceptance, resilience, and commitment.

Dr. David Petrovay's book gives the reader a deeper understanding about the process of career transition through self reflection exercises. He facilitates a thorough process of looking at key issues for those in career transition to be able to strengthen and develop critical life tools--one's self-confidence, perseverance, acceptance, resilience, commitment, and support.

*To Ronald V. Kardashian for his
constant support and belief in me during this journey*

Acknowledgments

A presentation that I gave to a group of job seekers in April 2013 on dealing with the challenges of being unemployed became the seed that germinated into this book. The focus of the presentation was on the psychological aspects of unemployment and how to cope with change and transition. My thanks to Sharon and Larry Staley, the event organizers, for that opportunity. The attendees were quite vocal in what it was like for each of them as they experienced the highs and lows that accompanied their efforts to secure a new job. I accumulated first-hand knowledge of the pains and problems they experienced, and at the end of the evening, I asked myself what I should do with what I had learned.

I knew that this intimate knowledge obtained from those participants was important and that with it came an opportunity to present to other groups on this topic and to validate what I had heard. There were five elements that surfaced as I presented through the following years. I was faced with a decision on what to do. If I continued to share what I had learned through my programs at a local level, I would reach no more than a hundred people per program. I soon saw a greater need to share this with so many people who were going through this unemployment experience. Thus was born the idea of writing a book.

The only other project of this magnitude that I had encountered was writing my doctoral dissertation. That was a simpler task because it was formulaic. A book required me to expand on the ideas that my audiences had shared with me in a manner that would not only inform but also educate people on tools they could incorporate into their lives to survive changes in their work status.

After speaking to several people who had authored various genres of books, I chose to hire my first writing coach. What was to be a one-year effort in preparing a book for publication stretched to seven years. Had it not been for Eve Visconti, my writing coach, I'm not sure a book would have ever materialized. Eve guided me through the writing process, allowing me to stay focused on a finished product. When I knew that Eve had given me enough motivation and feedback to begin my book, I enlisted the services of Maggi Kirkbride. Maggi guided me to the next level of my writing. She has been my constant source of inspiration and perseverance to have my book published.

Once I completed my first draft, I sought volunteers to read through it and provide feedback on their thoughts and impressions. My thanks to Sheri Bortz, Vicki Brown, Judy MacLaren, Nancy Merchant, Vic Ortiz, Mary Lynne Schoenbeck, Larry Staley, Ron Visconti, Bob Wohlsen, Julie Wright and Theresa Zieniewicz for their time in reviewing the manuscript.

As I approached the final stages of publication I reached out to my colleague, Eve Delunas, for her suggestions on how to get my book into the hands of those who would benefit from its message. Her recommendation to hire an editor led me to Jean Boles, who offered her professional expertise to complete the project. I have learned that it takes a village to publish a book.

Contents

Foreword

Is there life between jobs? Dr. David Petrovay not only answers the question YES, but he also gives you tangible actions to better support you in succeeding on your journey to gainful employment. You not only will better appreciate and understand yourself while preparing for your next opportunity, but you will also gain added purpose and direction that can carry you well throughout life.

When I first met David, I was intrigued by not only his depth of knowledge and experience but also by his natural manner of effective communication. He has a very effective way of engaging

you in conversations while stimulating your thought processes and desire to further learn and grow. His book does the same.

Out of the gate, you are given thought-provoking exercises that help you reflect on your motivations, experiences, past accomplishments, and future goals. The tools provided go beyond the "read it and forget it". They are the epitome of experiential learning, motivating you to "read it, do it, and learn from it". There is a natural flow that helps you reflect and grow. If you are looking for a gentle read that lets you off the hook with an easy formula to get you hired, then I would recommend you look elsewhere. If you are looking for a resource that helps you understand yourself, your abilities, your motivations, your successes, and your future potential, then you're in the right place! Combined with the available workbook, this is a very effective 1-2 punch in jumpstarting your journey!!

Finding a new role is more than just sending out resumes, interviewing, and accepting the offer given to you. It should be so easy! David walks you through the emotional stresses and strains that come along with change and leads you down a path to not only accepting their inevitability but to thriving during the transition. The solid ideas presented inspire you to face the facts. The self-analysis tools and exercises bring increased awareness. You learn to accept the things that might be immovable, appreciate the positives you have, and move on to implement the changes that will set you up for success.

I like the holistic approach to all aspects of the job search process covered in the book's pages. Physical, emotional, and psychological considerations are well-covered. You are walked through the process, clearly and methodically, in a way that allows you to explore your motivations. The ultimate result is one of self-understanding, which prepares you to understand and pursue the opportunities that surround you. When you answer the questions proposed honestly, you develop a better understanding of who you are and the nature of your why, which then opens doors to a deeper understanding of your motivations and capabilities that plays to your strengths. The enhanced confidence gained allows you to know, understand, and then pursue your dreams to the fullest. It is refreshing to not be told what to do, but to be stimulated into understanding your why, which then lets you proceed down the path appropriate specifically for you.

You can tell that David has deep educational roots with a firm foundation in psychology. He stimulates the senses while enhancing your awareness as he walks you through various experiential learning opportunities that get to the core of why you do what you do and how to do it better. I have rarely seen a concept like gratitude discussed in a career self-help book, but that is only one of the ideas that are covered that can lead you to effective outcomes in your career search journey. Even topics like humor and resilience, along with pressure and uncertainty help you appreciate the realities of the search process, and in turn, help you to better cope with the challenges and opportunities along the way.

Sprinkled with a variety of inspirational quotes that hit the mark and introduce most sections, the content presented is also inspirational and worthy of being quoted itself. You are assisted in defining and executing your priorities. If you seek career success and growth, reading and applying the lessons learned can carry you forward. This tome puts you on the right path to understanding your own goals and achieving them.

David, appreciate the insights you share and the inspiration you provide!

Dr. Scott Dell

Introduction

Many of us believe that what we do defines who we are. As children, we were often asked, "What do you want to be when you grow up?" The answers ranged from firefighter to ballerina to astronaut. It would be highly unlikely that a child would respond to the question with, "When I grow up, I want to be unemployed." As time passed we most likely changed our ideas about what our careers would look like. This was based on knowing more of who we were as it related to our interests, values, skills, and personality. New experiences became the basis for new directions.

Career paths rarely follow a straight line. For many, the belief that the occupation for which they had trained would fill their work years. That became my own mindset, and it was used to survive any changes that took place during my decades of work. The transitions accompanying the changes that did take place weren't always as smooth as planned. There were times when one job flowed effortlessly into another, and there were times when life felt more like a roller coaster with no end in sight.

My models for dealing with those changes were members of my immediate family. Growing up in the 50s and 60s, the expectation was that you chose an occupation and stayed with it until retirement. That meant committing more than 40 years to doing the same type of work. You didn't necessarily have to like what you did for a living; you only had to do what was needed to keep your job long enough to earn a pension. Then you could relax for the next 20 years or so, accounting to no one but yourself.

My journey on this path began upon completing my degree at the University of Pittsburgh coupled with a decision as to what the next step would be. It was 1970 and the Vietnam War was still raging. The graduation ceremonies scheduled for April unexpectedly coincided with my draft notice along with a letter from the Graduate School of Education. The letter was a solicitation for college graduates to consider becoming special education teachers. There was a severe shortage of teachers at the time and fellowships were available to cover schooling. My only plan for proceeding was to meet with the head of each program specialty to determine which one might work for me. It wasn't until a meeting with the last professor in the department that my plan unfolded. "I could do that job."

My admission to graduate school was contingent upon the results of my eligibility to be drafted. Armed with only a five-by-five-inch slip of paper from my doctor explaining that there was a history of knee dislocations, the march from station to station commenced. Since the person in line before me had submitted an entire packet as he was inducted, my chances of being denied were thought to be narrow to slim. When the officer surprisingly said to me, "Sorry; we can't take you," it was off to graduate school to learn how to teach children with visual impairments.

This next step was highly accelerated. Since the need for teachers was so great, the program was designed to deliver a master's degree in eight months, with an additional quarter to compensate for the credits lacked in not being an undergraduate education major. The first transition related to work arrived, and it turned out to be easier than expected. While doing my student teaching, the principal of the school approached me and asked if I had plans following my completion of the program. She told me that if I hadn't any, she would like for me to apply to work there.

After successfully going through the interview process, my first professional job awaited me. That September, a classroom of 13 students with visual impairments and other disabilities was assigned to me. It didn't take long before realizing that my formal training prepared me little for what lay ahead. If it hadn't been for the inherent programming that you stick with the job no matter what happens, that first year of teaching would have ended with a letter of resignation.

Following that initial year, the transitions between work assignments were somewhat easier. After seven years in my first teaching job, a similar position opened in Arizona. Being accepted necessitated a move across the country. My travels had never been any farther than five hours from my home. This was my first major experience with the psychological aspects of a job change; it meant leaving my support system and all that had been familiar for almost 30 years.

After my 22 years employed as a teacher, a career development specialist, and an assistant principal at the same school in Arizona, the option for full retirement became available, and it was time to take advantage of that opportunity. The decision to leave, especially with a job offer in California, felt right. Again, the transition was a smooth one.

The next five years coupled my work as an educator with my work on my doctorate at the University of Arizona. At the end of those five years, another hard question arose: "Is this how you want to spend the next ten or more years of your life?" Since a second pension was an option, it took only a few moments for the answer to come to me—NO. Within a short time, my letter of resignation was sitting on the desk of the superintendent with no clear-cut plan as to what to do next. It felt like hitting the wall at 200 miles an hour and its impact left me reeling. Thus far my career path was largely the result of happenstance rather than conscious planning.

There was no longer the desire to work in education. What next? It harkened back to the days of selecting my college major. When speaking to prospective employers, all they could see was an educator. What words would convince them that I could be otherwise? This became my period of rediscovery. It began by joining a professional networking group that allowed me to experiment with different jobs. Among them was career coaching. The feedback received from those around me was positive. It reminded me how much enjoyment there was in helping others. Much of what was involved in this type of work tapped into my eight years as a career development specialist in the school, so it wasn't like starting from scratch. Thank goodness for transferable skills!

Through this networking group came the opportunity for informational interviews which led to a position with a nonprofit that provided career services to adults with disabilities. My 34 years of working with such individuals provided the necessary background. At the same time, my dissertation required to complete my doctoral studies was coming to an end. With this came the realization that there would be little opportunity for advancement. The good news was that my current experience would allow me to apply for other similar positions, ones with more career advancement opportunities. This led to being hired to work for a one-stop career center where my skills could be fine-tuned. After working there for almost two years, my doctoral program was over. It was time to make another job change that would require me to rethink my career path.

Approaching 60, the next step was a decision to go into business for myself. This would afford me a flexible schedule and the freedom to travel. The first few years were a struggle. There were months with only one client scheduled. This was the time to focus my attention on how to develop my professional skills and knowledge. It meant taking time to register for online classes, participate in professional organizations, and learn how to network for self-marketing.

It would be comforting to think that the changes in my life related to my work have now reached an endpoint. That is not the case. New opportunities lead to new transitions. *I have learned that with age comes resilience—knowing that one can survive changes. I have written this book to share how changes and the transitions accompanying them can be addressed in positive ways.*

In my many years as a career coach working with over a thousand individuals in both individual and group settings, specific themes regarding the psychological aspects of work became apparent to me. While the need to learn job search skills such as interviewing and networking was critical to the process, success in moving forward was strongly associated with the person's ability to handle transitions. One client might demonstrate the ability to competently respond to content in interview questions and lack the self-confidence needed to effectively communicate that to the interviewer. Another client may be trapped in feelings of betrayal after working for a company for over twenty years and then being told in an email that the position was being eliminated.

Regardless of what you are seeking, whether it be the next job or changing to a new field, there are five elements that emerge that support success in surviving the period between jobs when one enters the world of uncertainty. These elements are derived from an open-ended question that I posed to a group of job seekers during a panel discussion. When asked to name topics that were pertinent to their current situation and what would be helpful in finding employment, they identified five traits. These common threads show up among the hundreds of individual clients and the thousands of job seekers encountered as part of my work as a career counselor and coach. These are the five key elements that you can apply to survive life's challenges and to achieve what you desire in life, including a job that matches your talents and interests. These five elements are **self-confidence, perseverance, acceptance, resilience**, and **commitment**.

The words in this book also serve as a reflection on my own personal transitions related to work. The old adage of practicing what you preach comes into play here—it would have been much easier if I had used the tools outlined in the book during those changes in my life!

Our formal education provides for a strong knowledge base in the arts and sciences, but it often lacks instruction in how to cope with changes. Most of that instruction comes from observation of those around us. If you're lucky enough to be surrounded by people who handle change in a positive way, then you're likely to have a model for what that would look like for you. If you did not have such people in your life, or if there were gaps, this book will assist you in learning ways to navigate through the uncertainties of change.

At the beginning of each chapter is a short self-assessment designed to provide you with a sense of where you currently stand related to the topic at hand. These are not formalized instruments with standardized test scores, since there are no right or wrong answers, but rather they are a series of **Yes** or **No** statements, generated based on the content of the chapter. If you find that you scored **Low** in a particular area, you may want to begin your focus on that related chapter. As you complete each of the assessments, date them, and retake the assessment at some future time after you have had an opportunity to implement the tools in the chapter. Note the changes in your responses and take time to identify the factors and events that have contributed to those changes.

Included in the chapters are exercises within each of the headings that are designed to further develop the tools by providing a clearer understanding of what you're hoping to achieve. The more clarity you have, the more likely your success will be in formulating a plan that you can accomplish. Write your responses on the pages provided. The exercises can help you integrate the ways that you have been successful in navigating past transitions with ones that you're experiencing now.

The quotations that accompany each of the sections come from a variety of sources that span centuries, reminding you that change and transition have been with us since man first walked on this Earth. These quotations represent the thoughts of philosophers, athletes, writers, politicians, and people like you and me. There are also statements from individuals who have recently experienced a change in job status and their thoughts and feelings around the transition accompanying it. To protect their confidentiality, only their initials are used, and these may be altered at the request of the contributor. In some cases, the occupation of the individual was included based upon their preferences.

This message contained within these pages is not about a guaranteed road to fame and fortune. For me, there are always thoughts and feelings of being wary whenever the word "guaranteed" is associated with any service or product. There is no magic formula as to how you can rise from destitution and poverty to becoming a millionaire rubbing elbows with the jet set by following seven simple steps. The road to success is built by you alone. It may be based on your financial goals, a specific lifestyle, or your contribution to a cause in which you strongly believe. The good news is that the definition of success is directly correlated to the number of inhabitants of the planet today. Congratulate yourself on reading this book and completing the exercises as a means to achieving your goals.

This book is not an academic exercise justifying the inclusion of the five elements described by the individuals who contributed to the content; it's a blueprint—a guide, a plan of action—to focus on the habits and discipline so each reader can develop to increase his or her use of that element. You may find that you already possess a high level of commitment or perseverance. You may want to focus on other areas that have been more of a challenge for you. Perhaps you need to bolster your self-confidence, or you may be wrestling with acceptance of your current situation. The chapters are not presented in hierarchical or linear form. You may start with Chapter Four and then move to Chapter Two based on what you learn from the assessments.

The purpose of this writing is to arm you with tools to fortify yourself during tough times. Some of the tools may be familiar to you, and this can be a reminder of their value. Others may be entirely new to you. All that is asked is that you be open to the possibility that, as they have helped others, they may also help you. Included in each of the chapters are statements from individuals from all walks of life offering testimony to how they have used each of the tools. My hope is that you will use this as a reference throughout your life whenever you find yourself facing difficult changes.

> *"I felt like I was going through a divorce (severance of a relationship) and a loss in my family. I was married to my job and when my position was eliminated, I felt like I lost my identity. My world changed in one day."*
> —AH Principal, Customer Engagement Specialist

CHAPTER ONE

Transition and Change

"The only thing that is constant is change."
—Heraclitus

Transitions self-assessment quiz

In preparation for the chapter that follows, please complete the following assessment based on the thoughts and feelings that you're having today. Remember that there are no right or wrong answers.

Mark **Yes** or **No** as it applies to your life today.

1. I find it easy to deal with changes in my life.	Yes	No
2. I seek out the advice of people I trust when I am going through a transition.	Yes	No
3. I think back over the circumstances that brought about a change and consider alternative ways I could have dealt with it.	Yes	No
4. I see change as an opportunity.	Yes	No
5. I realize that the strong emotions I feel in reaction to changes in my life are temporary.	Yes	No
6. I generally maintain a positive attitude when I am going through a change.	Yes	No
7. I know that I can survive a change based on prior experience.	Yes	No
8. I feel like I am in control of my life most of the time.	Yes	No
9. I can empathize with others who are going through changes in their lives.	Yes	No
10. I am aware of how I deal with transitions in my life.	Yes	No

To determine your score, count the number of **Yes** statements. ____

8-10 You indicate a **high** degree of ability within this area.

4-7 You indicate a **moderate** degree of ability within this area.

1-3 You indicate a **low** degree of ability within this area.

My father was born in 1924. During the many years that he worked, he held the same job position as a mail carrier. When he retired, he had held that job for over 40 years. My mother stayed at home and raised four children. Women who chose to do this were referred to as "housewives." When asked if the choices they made were aligned with the dreams they held in their late teens and early 20s, each parent expressed regret for what might have been. *Neither one ever shared their career aspirations.* They quietly accepted what they believed to be the fate they had been handed.

This bears mentioning because it demonstrates how our attitude toward work and employment has changed through the generations. This attitude was not unusual for my parents' generation, based on their educational level and societal expectations. Work provided a steady source of income and offered a sense of security for people across classes. This attitude toward work did not change much from the time that my parents were employable to when my career began in the early 1970s. This was the start of the baby boomer generation, comprising about 76 million individuals born from 1946 to 1964.

The amount of time spent working in a single position has changed. Nowadays the median time spent in one job is about 4.4 years. Job positions can change as many as ten times during one's lifetime. For each subsequent generation, the overall number of jobs held increases. This means that individuals will experience job changes more frequently, undergoing a transition with each change.

It's important to differentiate between a change and a transition. **Change is situational.** It's brought about by some external event such as the birth of a child or a new job. The event brings forth a new set of circumstances that significantly differ from the way life was before the event occurred. **Transition is a psychological response to the change that has occurred**. While change appears to be one-dimensional, transition covers multiple responses to the event. For example, if a change in employment requires relocating to a new city, there will also be an adjustment to forming new relationships, establishing new routines, and identifying resources for common services such as car repair and medical care.

What we know is that the natural progression during change begins with an *end*. That which was is no longer. It may be a divorce, the death of a parent, or becoming unemployed. All of these are events and are devoid of specific emotional content, per se. What may be the source of fear and confusion for one person may be seen as hopeful

> *"Anger, shame, social loss. When I lost my position I was mad at my manager. Later, I felt self-pity. I also lost some close friends as part of this transition."*
> —JP, Customer Success Manager

or exciting to another during the change. The *ending* is followed by a period when the individual may experience a lack of clarity or depression regarding the future. This often correlates to the amount of time before a new beginning appears on the horizon. In the case of a transition between jobs, there may be periods of self-doubt, guilt, anger, and despair. Hopefully, the situation changes and a new chapter begins.

The changes that occur within the workplace can be attributed to many sources. The 21st century is riddled with mergers and acquisitions, outsourcing, and globalization. Closer to home is downsizing, reorganization, and the demise of companies who outlived their usefulness in the marketplace. On a more personal level, there are transfers, layoffs, promotions, terminations, and simply the desire to leave one setting in search of new opportunities. Such changes can affect thousands of workers or be singular in their impact.

One significant source of change affecting workers across all generations today is automation. Work tasks such as those involved in mining and manufacturing are subject to performance by machines such as robots.

These automated workers have no need for breaks, shift assignments, family leave, insurance, or cost of living pay increases. They are capable of working non-stop on a 24/7/365 basis. The concept of driverless cars, which will have a dramatic impact on jobs such as taxi drivers, is being researched. As occupational tasks become automated, human workers would be displaced requiring them to seek new opportunities. How would a large sector of unskilled or semiskilled workers find new employment? What does this mean in terms of the transitions they will experience during this time of flux?

It's important to realize that we deal with change constantly as part of life. It's inevitable. My own life, like that of most people, has been a constant series of transitions on both a personal and professional level. These changes begin at birth and continue in ways that are hardly noticeable. There are changes that occur on a physiological level as you learn to crawl, stand, walk, run, and further develop fine (small movements) and gross (larger movements) motor skills. There are changes related to your mental capacities as your thinking moves from concrete to abstract concepts. You also become increasingly aware of the role that your emotions play in your life and how to cope with them. Each change requires an adjustment in how you function in the world. These are the transitions that determine how well you will adapt to what comes next.

> *"After my recent job loss I felt a bit of sadness but at the same time hope for the future. I was grateful for my time and experience at the company. I didn't want to stay there employed much longer because of low morale and was looking for other opportunities prior to my release."*
> —ED, Business Analyst

Exercise: Write the events that marked transitions in your life at the appropriate points on the timeline. They can include graduations, starting your first job, marriage, birth of a child, promotion at work, and so on.

—0

—10

—20

—30

—40

—50

—60

—70

What was most important to you at this time?

Were you successful in achieving it?

What did you do to generate that success?

What could you have done differently?

When the transition is associated with the work that you do, it's important to draw upon your prior success in handling change. Can the changes that occur stimulate new ways of approaching uncharted territory?

> *"My initial feeling was shock. I also felt betrayal, disappointment. What I did immediately was launch a job search. I began interviewing for jobs within a few weeks of getting let go. I was optimistic that I was in high demand and would land a great role. As those and many other opportunities have come and gone, I am left with a lack of hope. I find HOPE is what we need most at this time."*
> —JW, Director of Marketing

If coping with change has been a challenge for you, what can you do differently to affect a positive outcome? While your first inclination may be to blame the people or circumstances around you, in the long run it will do little to alter what has occurred. Granted that it's necessary to work through your initial reactions to what has happened. You may deny the effect that the change will have on you and then have a sense of anger over the perceived disruption to your life. These are natural responses to major changes. It's when you allow them to take over your life that they can become problematic.

Once you recognize the inevitability of change that is occurring in your life, you can consciously choose the next steps in your transition. This requires that you accept that it's time to take charge of your life and move forward. This involves taking on a proactive role in your career. In my own experience with change and transition, the lesson learned was that one could ill afford to spend significant amounts of time trying to change external events that led to the current status. Oftentimes this meant reading the writing on the wall prior to the event presenting itself and beginning to plan my course of action. One case in particular was a conversation I had with my supervisor after meeting a new superintendent. A feeling of apprehension and foreboding was pervasive while telling her that something was amiss. In less than a year neither of us was still in our original position. Creating an exit plan following that meeting allowed me to feel more in control of the situation.

One benefit of change and the transition that accompanies it is that it provides you with an opportunity to learn more about yourself. It allows for introspection as to what matters in future decisions. How did the work that you performed support your value system and your personality type? How much did you have to compromise about

> *"It is most unfortunate my hiring manager was transitioned to a different role and I had a new manager. The work style and expectations are not what I signed up for."*
> —ML, IT Management

who you are to function in the workplace? How important is it that the culture in which you work is compatible with how you see yourself? One way to recognize whether this compatibility exists is by asking yourself questions like, "Did I fit in?" and "Did I like working there?" If the answer is, "no," look at the disconnect and what is contributing to that. How can you use this information when choosing your next job?

Perhaps in your prior position you felt isolated from co-workers whereas you normally thrive on interaction. Maybe you didn't believe in the direction the company was taking after it had been acquired by another company. It could have been that there was an informal network that thrived on gossip or that there was an expectation that your team would celebrate the end of the week by partying with heavy drinking when you don't drink. Transitions are a time to consider what worked and didn't work and plan accordingly.

Exercise: Now consider the transitions that you experienced during your career. They may or may not be based on what you wrote on your timeline. Begin with a specific **event,** such as starting a new job in the past, and be sure to write what it was. Next, identify what your **response** was to the event. It might be that you were looking forward to the change, had questions about the nature of the work you would be doing, etc. Now list the **emotions** you felt related to the event: hopeful, excited, worried, doubt, etc. What **memories** did you have related to the event? What was the **outcome** of the change and the transition that accompanied it? Finally, what did you **learn** about yourself as a result of it?

Career

Event ____

____

Response ____

____

____

____

Emotions attached to event ________________________________

____

____

____

Memories of event ____

____

____

____

Outcome(s)____

____

____

____

Learnings ____

____

____

____

The challenges of change

"In the middle I want to be at the end,
at the end I want to be in the beginning,
and in the beginning I want to be in bed."
—Jarod Kintz

When a person has a change in job status, any one of a number of emotions emerge. For many, frustration, bewilderment, confusion, panic, betrayal, and anxiety are but a few of the feelings that surface once the reality of what has occurred sets in. Questions of how to pay your bills, how to find your next job, and whether or not someone would be willing to hire you contribute to a downward spiral of emotions and negative selftalk. For some, this can be a time for feeling displaced; for others, this is a time of anticipation, hope, and excitement.

> *"[I felt] anger, depression anxiety... How, when, and where I will find a new job?"*
> —JP, Customer Success Manager

We have all heard of the proverbial "glass half full or glass half empty" metaphor as to how individuals approach the challenges that confront them. People use this filter to interpret the presence of such situations in their lives. Depending on whether their filter is positive or negative, it will frame the experience. Consider the following two scenarios.

Jack

Jack receives a pink slip as he leaves work on Friday. He has worked in this position for fifteen years and has performed at a level that is above satisfactory. His layoff comes as a shock to him and he drives home in a daze. His disbelief shifts into anger after arriving home. He wonders how this could have happened. He never saw it coming. He calls his best friend, Tom, and they arrange to meet so that he can vent about the events of the day. In the course of the conversation, Jack begins to talk about the red flags that should have alerted him that his job was on the line. He sees how attending to these clues could have saved his job. Tom offers his support to help Jack begin to think through his options as to what to do next. Jack shares how he always wanted to work more with his hands rather than sit at a computer terminal all day. This could be an opportunity to explore doing exactly that type of work.

> *"I think the change in job status can bring forth new challenges and new opportunities."*
>
> — AW

Bill

Bill works at the same company as Jack. He also is handed a pink slip as he leaves work on Friday. When he realizes what it is, he immediately reacts with a string of expletives. "How could they do this to me?" He drives to the local bar and drowns the news with four vodka double martinis. He finally arrives home at 2:00 AM and drags himself off to bed. He spends the rest of the weekend planning his revenge for how the company treated him, even though he would never carry out that plan. It felt good to use this plotting as a means of gaining a sense of control. Three more vodka double martinis helped to anesthetize his anger, at least temporarily. Right now the future looks rather bleak to Bill, with no prospect of how to change it in sight.

While these two scenarios represent opposite ends of the continuum, they offer the opportunity to ask yourself, "Which is more likely the way I would respond to such a situation?" Most of us find ourselves somewhere between Jack and Bill. Ask yourself which one of these men is more likely to be healthier. Think back to the times when the Bill side of you was in control and consider what was happening with your blood pressure and your eating and sleeping habits. For Bill, the chances of entering into addictive behaviors increase. Situational depression may set in, further compounding the situation. The idea of getting out of bed in the morning to face the day becomes a source of inertia and distress.

> *"My initial emotional response was relief, happiness, and like a burden was lifted. I made too many sacrifices and stayed too long with hope for making it a better place."*
> – GW

People like Jack and Bill are faced with the uncertainties of employment. Workers in the 1950s were not concerned with practices such as offshoring, re-entry into the workforce following childrearing, the need to care for aging parents, replacing human labor with robots, outsourcing, and cyclical unemployment during a recession in which the supply of jobs is less than the demand. Workers of the 21st century need to keep abreast of the trends and skills needed as positions are phased out or redefined to remain competitive in the job market that is now global.

Before continuing, it's important to define some commonly used terms related to work. The terms include **career, field, occupation, and job.** While they may be used interchangeably, they are not the same.

Your **career** is the sum total of all that you do. The word *career* is derived from the 16th-century French word *carriere,* meaning *road.* Roads twist and turn to accommodate the terrain. They are made up of detours, dead ends, and intersections. We consciously choose the next direction based on what lies before us. Your career is more than the specific jobs you hold in much the same way that a road is more than the section of pavement beneath it. Today people are changing jobs much more frequently than they did at the turn of the twentieth century. After almost 50 years of employment, my **career** continues until I retire.

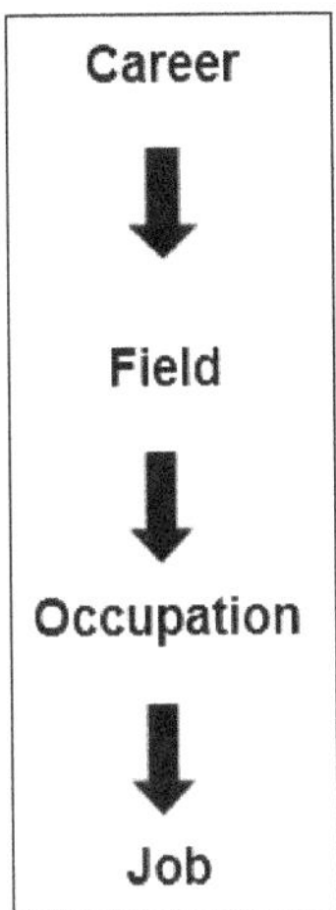

Your **field** refers to the industry that a career encompasses. Among the fields you could pursue could be arts and entertainment, communications, business, health and medicine, or government. For example, people could be in the *environmental* career field. This is not their actual job title. Their job title would be specific to their duties, such as forester or environmental engineer. Each of these fields requires a different set of skills and training. One of my longest periods of employment with a single company was 22 years. During that time I held four different, very distinct positions, all within the **field** of education.

Occupations are a subset of the larger construct of career. Your occupation is a position that involves specific training needed to perform expected tasks for which financial compensation is provided. This might be a doctor, a carpenter, or a teacher. People may remain in the same occupation or make several occupational changes during their work life. We narrowly think of work as the position in which we are currently employed, most often referred to as our occupation. When a person changes a position, a time of transition accompanies it.

Your **job** is a piece of work that you perform for pay. It includes the specific tasks required for that position. This is what is typically outlined in a job description. In the case of teacher, it may be to plan and deliver lessons, track grades, maintain classroom discipline, communicate with parents, and monitor the playground. Jobs have a shelf life based on the needs of both the organization and the individual. Among today's millennial generation (those born from 1980-2000) the average time spent in one job may be less than two years. We need to think beyond the 9 to 5 jobs that were so much a part of what was considered traditional employment and adopt a more comprehensive view of what work entails.

Affirmation:

I welcome the challenges that come with change, knowing that with each step I take, I am aligning myself closer to a fulfilling and rewarding future.

Applying transitions to your career path

"Life is one big transition."
– Willie Stargell

When did your career path and the transitions that accompanied it begin? Your career path began the day you accepted your first job. That could have been delivering newspapers, babysitting, or mowing the neighbor's lawn. It was the first time you accepted money in exchange for the tasks you performed. For me, it was working in a concession stand in an amusement park following my high school graduation in 1966. The pay was $0.90 an hour with a $0.10 bonus for each of the hours worked until the end of the season. Since hard work was not foreign to me, the transition from school to employment was not that difficult. Within a few weeks, there was a promotion to manager of our concession stand. At 17 my job duties included closing out the registers, ordering food and supplies, and scheduling those who worked in our stand. There was quite a bit to be learned from that experience.

My summers between my college studies were filled with jobs such as a warehouse worker in a research and development company, a landscaper, and an assembly line worker in a soft drink manufacturing company. How did each of these jobs fit into my career path? Each job was invaluable in understanding the nature of work as it applies to my position as a career counselor and coach. Each of those jobs had a short shelf life given that they lasted no more than three or four months before returning to school. The short duration of each job impressed the importance of being a quick learner since the expectation was to demonstrate competence in my job within a week.

Because most of the jobs held in my early years involved repetitive tasks, the tasks surrounding them did not require sophisticated skill sets. This is generally true for most people as they begin their careers. The skills that were used in one setting could be applied to the next job held. Manual dexterity, tolerating repetition, following directions, and thoroughness were common threads in performing my job duties. These skills are what are commonly referred to as transferable skills. They cross work settings and allow for easier transitions since they are already familiar. As time passes and new employment opportunities present themselves, additional skills come into play. In my role as a teacher my ability to plan, evaluate, report, observe, and listen was strengthened. Longevity in this role reinforced these abilities until they became transferable skills. All of these are critical skills in my work as a career counselor and coach today.

Exercise: On the following page, make a list of each of the jobs you have performed in your life. Next to each job, write the skills that you developed that were transferable to future positions. A list of skills is provided in the **Appendix** at the end of this book to use as a reference.

Job Description	Transferable Skills

In addition to the skills you developed, you also viewed work as a reflection of the values you held. Values are beliefs or ideals that tend to be enduring throughout life. They are generally shared by the members of a culture or generation about what is desirable and undesirable. Values serve as guides when making decisions about situations in your life. Perhaps one of the values you hold is honesty. You will most likely react to situations in which those around you choose to do otherwise. During a transition, it will be important to consider those values in the opportunities that become available to you. Would accepting a position that involved an unethical behavior or falsifying information on your resume or application support your value of honesty? How are the values that you hold dear demonstrated in the work you do?

> *"I thought I was doing a phenomenal job executing on all the priorities. I delivered and made all the deadlines. Why does management no longer think I am a good fit?"*
> — ML, IT Management

When asked what is most important in a future job, a common response among those in the baby boomer generation (those born from 1946-1964) is *security*. This is a value based on the work ethic they learned when entering the workforce in the 1960s. Their belief was that loyalty to a company would be returned in kind. This loyalty translated into remaining with the company under any conditions so that you would eventually qualify for a pension that would help sustain you in your so-called "golden years."

Fast forward into the 21st century and you realize how much that belief is being tested. If you follow any of the news related to business trends, you see that down-sizing, outsourcing, telecommuting, globalization, and restructuring are today's buzzwords. Many of the large corporations of the 60s and 70s no longer exist. Names like Woolworths, Pan Am Airlines, and General Foods Corporation were once common household names. Today they are only memories, taking with them thousands upon thousands of jobs.

Each generation typically shares values and viewpoints based upon the circumstances that surround them. These values and viewpoints influence the lifestyles and attitudes toward work and career. Judgments and misunderstandings arise when members of one generation find themselves working alongside a member of another generation. This may also affect how generations experience transitions. The values held by one generation may appear to be foreign to another. What is important to recognize is that none of them represents an ideal upon which the others should model themselves.

The chart below may help in clarifying some of the characteristics of the generations currently in the workplace. Remember that these are generalizations and do not describe every individual within that generation.

Related Subject	Traditionalists	Baby Boomers	Generation X	Millennials
Birth Years	1900-1945	1946-1964	1965-1980	1980-2000
Numbers	49 million	76 million	46 million	75 million
Career Development:	Work is a given Company loyalty	Upward mobility Stable employment over time	Continuous learning both inside and outside the organization Loyalty to self rather than to company	Requests for more experience and opportunities Willing to look beyond work for experience
View of Time:	Time clocks Work until the job is finished	Workaholics Physical presence in the workplace required	Project oriented Payment for project completion	Work is what you do between weekends A flexible schedule Work hard until 5:00
The work environment:	Recognition for experience Job security Clear rules and regulations	Employee of the month or year Being a good fit with the company mission Team work	Cutting edge technology Scheduling flexibility Meaningful tasks	Social networking Constant learning Want to be challenged
Retirement:	Retire after 30 years with a livable pension	My work is my identity so I need to work at least part-time	I want to experience variety in life and so I may change fields	I am not sure what retirement will look like and will defer what that looks like for now

Exercise: What is most important to you in the work that you do? It may be security, financial compensation, skills development, education, working as a team, or fame. Think back to the work you have done in the past as well as the work you currently do. What motivates you most to get up and go to work? In the space below list the five most critical aspects of what you seek in the work you do. These can be used to determine if an employment opportunity is right for you as a source of satisfaction.

1. ____

____

2. ____

____

3. ____

____

4. ____

____

5. ____

____

As an individual seeking new employment opportunities either voluntarily or involuntarily, you face options as to how to proceed. Having a college degree is no longer a guarantee of being hired, nor is working for the same company for 20 years a statement of your worth and value. You're linked to your presence on social media and the breadth of your network. You are cautioned to think carefully for posting on any of the various social media available to you since potential employers will research your online postings, especially if they contain references to behaviors that might affect workplace performance. A posting about that wild weekend you spent in Las Vegas may not stay in Vegas. Who you know may be just as, if not more, important than what you know.

Maintaining an active network connecting you to job opportunities is critical. It's estimated that somewhere between 60% and 80% of jobs for which people are hired are a result of active networking. Think of previous jobs you have held and the role that networking played in being hired. There is also the extensive online research you conduct in choosing which company to apply and preparing your interview responses. Resumes no longer consist of a laundry list of the duties you performed, but now are statements of how you can make a difference for the company that hires you.

Affirmation:

I approach transitions with optimism and excitement, seeing each circumstance as an opportunity to learn, grow, and evolve.

Approaches to transition

How individuals approach change and transition varies considerably. Consider the job seeker who might contact me as a career counselor stating, "I have been out of work for six months now, and I need help in figuring out what type of job I should be applying for. I haven't really been satisfied with what I've done in the past, and I am hoping that you can assist me in what to do next." While this is a common way that the career counseling process begins, what follows can vary greatly in how the client approaches the changes he or she is experiencing at the moment.

> *"What am I going to do now?*
> *Who and what do I want to be?*
> *So many options. Where do I go from here?"*
> — GW

From my experience, there are five types of clients who venture into that first meeting.

The Dreamer

This individual may be feeling pressure from a spouse or a parent to take some form of action to find a job. Or perhaps their financial resources are being exhausted and there is a need to find anything that would cover their living expenses. Or there has been a major change in lifestyle, such as a divorce, that compels them to rejoin the workforce after a lengthy period of unemployment. There can be a sense of urgency that presents itself as we meet. "I'll take anything that comes along." But as we talk, this presents itself as only a half-truth. The person is more selective than what they state in their plea for work. Often, the salary and the job duties outlined are only remotely aligned with reality.

There is usually a request to review their resume which may contain references to two or three disparate job titles. Their hope is that something on their resume will catch the eye of the reviewer leading to a call for an interview. They are asked to think about what it would be like to be at the reading end of the resume and the amount of time it would take to determine what type of position this individual would fill within the company. When given the option to spend some time identifying a position that matches their skills, interests, and experience, they agree that this would be a worthwhile plan. A typical conversation may go like this:

Client: "I have been doing the same type of work now for 15 years, and I think it's time for a change."

Coach: "What have you been thinking about doing in your next job?"

Client: "I want to make a lot of money, and I think that going into real estate would be a good way to do that. I like looking at houses."

Coach: "What do you know about being a realtor?"

Client: "You take a test and then you start to sell homes. All it takes is selling one home a year and you have enough to live on."

Coach: "Do you know anyone who works in the real estate business?" Client: "No."

Coach: "It would be helpful to speak to a realtor to learn what it takes to become established in the field."

Client: "Sure. I could do that."

Coach: "Let's talk about how to go about setting that up."

The session proceeds and the client has a plan to contact a realtor to gather information about the steps needed to gain entry into the field and the challenges of starting out from square one as opposed to working with an established family member or colleague with a proven track record. So the person leaves armed with a strategy for determining if becoming a realtor would be feasible and a return date for reporting what he has learned. Time passes with no subsequent communication from them.

The Rationalizer

Then there is the individual who is seeking a job change because of their situation in their current job. They are feeling pressured by job demands or don't think that their supervisor recognizes their contributions. They cringe when they imagine having to interact with the person to whom they report. "If I could just find a place to work where my boss understood me better or I didn't have so many assignments that were outside my interests." We meet for several sessions to identify their needs and how they could be met in their current or future position. After making progress they inform me that things have changed at work. It might be that the supervisor or coworker who made life there intolerable is no longer employed in that department. A typical conversation might proceed like this:

Coach: "When we first started meeting you told me how difficult it was to work with your boss. You were seriously considering other employment. How is that going?"

Client: "You know. I have thought about it and it really isn't as bad as I described it. I like my coworkers and I would miss them."

Coach: "So what have you decided about staying in your current position?"

Client: "I'll see how things go over the next six months and get back to you should anything change."

Now that the obstacle appears to have been removed or minimized, it isn't really so bad at work. They convince themselves that they can tough it out, so there is no need to continue working together. They have created a rationalization that will keep them tied to this position. Should circumstances change, they will be in touch with me. That rarely occurs.

Sometimes there is a change in command and this allows for some breathing time with the hope that perhaps this relationship will be healthier than the one before it. The person is confident that he or she will be much more aware of landmines should they surface. "I'll call you for an appointment if things change." For months and even years, there is little contact between us. A client may eventually reconnect when the work situation becomes intolerable or they are let go. It's at this time that they realize how little progress they have made in their professional growth and the precious time that was wasted.

The need to cover everyday living expenses can become overwhelming, and so the first job offer that is presented is the one that is taken. There is little time spent weighing the pros and cons of the choice being made. "It seemed to be a good offer at the time, but I didn't really ask for specifics other than knowing what the salary and benefits would be." They feel like they have little recourse in approaching the individual who hired them to clarify the duties and expectations for the work they are doing. They have painted themselves into a corner and now believe they have to live with the consequences of their decision.

The Validator

This individual arrives without any type of short or long-term goal in working together. They come with a specific question for which they are seeking an immediate answer. Our conversation may sound something like this:

Client: "I am here because I want to make a decision as to which path to follow."

Coach: "What paths are you considering?"

Client: "Should I stay in my current job or look at pursuing a different field?"

Coach: "What would be the advantages and disadvantages of each path?"

During the session, we would explore those advantages and disadvantages. At the end of the session, the person would be clear on what the next step would be, or be close to making that decision. They see no need for additional meetings at that time, only to be resolute on where they are headed. He or she usually reports the results of their decision through informal follow up. They generally feel positive about their choice. There may be contact from them later on regarding a different decision they plan to make. In this case, there is a request to serve as a sounding board, allowing them to convince themselves as what future action to take.

The Deflector

This is an individual who will faithfully show up for their appointments and have nothing to show from their previous session. "I just didn't have time to work on the assignment. I had so many other things I needed to do. Maybe we can just talk about what I was supposed to work on." Or perhaps they call the day before the session to reschedule or cancel because they haven't accomplished anything. This type of person typically has other more pressing issues that require their attention. They may be going through situational depression that is affecting their ability to follow through with what they have committed to do. They may be feeling powerless over the conditions in their lives and relinquish that power to another, such as a coach. The coach is expected to work harder than they do. Then, when the expectations fail to transpire, the individual can blame the coach. Some leave the coaching relationship believing it had no value because their goal of finding a job never materialized. A typical conversation may go like this after two sessions:

Coach: "Let's review your tasks from our last session."

Client: "Well, I didn't really get much done."

Coach: "I know that our last session was several weeks ago. What was happening that kept you from your commitment to follow through on the tasks that we had agreed upon?"

Client: "My family decided to go on a vacation and that took up the time I would have been working on this."

Coach: "So what are your plans to complete the tasks?"

Client: "I have been thinking that maybe they aren't really going to help me move forward with my job search."

Coach: "What would you need for that to happen?"

Client: "I don't know. I was hoping that by now you would have identified the job I should be applying for. I guess this [career coaching] doesn't work."

In some cases, the person's needs go beyond my ability to provide the services best suited to address the most pressing problem. There may be other issues at hand, such as a disorder that requires professional support, or personal problems within a marriage that are sapping the client's time and energy. Once these needs are addressed the client may or may not return for coaching.

The Activator

Finally, there is the individual who consistently shows up as scheduled with either their assigned tasks in hand or they have sent them to me several days earlier for review. They are actively engaged in the process and often report on what they have done in addition to what we planned. "I found this great opportunity that I want to pursue. I've put together my cover letter and my resume, and I'd like you to review them and have you give me feedback. I've also been putting together a list of people I know to speak to about the position and how I can contribute to the growth of the company."

They believe they are in command of their career paths, and that is what they take into the workplace. They set specific goals and seek ways to ensure that they will achieve them. They may plan to sign up five new clients and report that they have exceeded their quota. They identify a position within their current company and work directly with their supervisors to find tasks that develop their skill sets, making them viable internal candidates for future openings. They think big and are willing to do what it takes to make their vision a reality.

They are constantly looking for future opportunities while at the same time assuming a realistic approach to their current position. They are keenly aware of both their strengths and their limitations. They know how to market their strong points and to develop ways to compensate for their weaknesses. Sharing accomplishments is a method for informing others of what they have been doing without it becoming an ego trip. They acknowledge their gifts and talents being utilized in the work setting. A typical conversation might sound like this:

Client: "I am really excited to tell you what I learned after leaving our last session."

Coach: "Tell me about it."

Client: "I contacted the people that I listed to learn more about opportunities in the field and what advice they might have for someone in my position."

Coach: "What advice did they have for you?"

Client: "They told me that it would be helpful to attend a local meeting of professionals and begin to build relationships with them. I already identified when and where the meetings are held and plan to attend the next one."

Coach: "How many people would you plan to speak to at the event and what will you do to follow through with them?"

Client: "I intend to speak to at least three people individually and exchange business contacts. I will then reach out to each of them within 24 hours as a way of building my network."

Minor setbacks do not paralyze them but serve as learning opportunities. After recovering from the initial problem, they accept responsibility for their part without taking on the victim or blaming role. It may be that there was a breakdown in communication and an assumption that someone was carrying out a critical task when they weren't. "I should have been more assertive in asking for clarification of what each of the team members was doing to ensure that nothing was left out." You will rarely hear "That wasn't my job" in reference to tasks that hadn't been completed. They assess the situation and determine what can be done to reduce the damage that has occurred.

Theirs is a sense of hopefulness about the future. They appear to be intrigued about possibilities, yet they would not be described as scattered or unfocused. They are determined to sort through their options to find the one that best suits the overall plan they have for life. A goal may be to gather experience working for various sized companies and eventually open their own business based on what they have learned. Or they may decide to learn the business from the bottom up so that they can take advantage of openings for advancement. For these people, the idea of creating and pursuing a five-year plan seems perfectly natural for them. Some begin with the end in mind while others take deliberate steps toward achieving their destination. They allow for current circumstances to effect adjustments to their plan without losing sight of where they are headed.

They seek balance and integration of the various aspects of their life. They are aware of how their health affects their ability to perform in the workplace. They know that the income from the work that they do supports a desired lifestyle. They appreciate the role that money plays and can broach the subject when needed. Life is not meant to be an ongoing financial struggle but an opportunity to embrace their value and how that is reflected in their bank account.

Lifelong learning is paramount in their career plan. They take advantage of online courses, webinars, trade publications and books written in their industry, and classes at local institutions of higher learning. "I just signed up for a software class." "I just completed a certification in gerontology." "I am watching a series of webinars on nonverbal communication skills." They are eager to share their learning with those around them and to apply their newfound knowledge in the workplace. They are never satisfied with knowing just enough to be passable. There is a thirst for information that can never be quenched. They take this thirst into other areas of their lives learning about their recreational interests as well as how to live healthier. They offer a balance of optimism and realism.

The following chart demonstrates where each of these five types of individuals would fit in their approach to their career paths based on their level of motivation and focus. The Dreamer requires clarity and direction. The Rationalizer needs to see how their acceptance of the status quo keeps them from moving forward in spite of their expressed desire to make changes. The Deflector benefits from facing the roadblocks and learning strategies for removing them. The Validator does well with evaluating the advantages and disadvantages of each of their options. The Activator will continue to advance with discussion and feedback on their progress.

	Unfocused	Focused
Low Motivation	The Dreamer	The Deflector
High Motivation	The Rationalizer	The Validator The Activator

Exercise: Which description best describes you at this point in your transition? What would it take for you to be more productive and proactive in your transition?

I most fit the description for Client Type________. For me to be more productive and proactive during my transition I would need to

Right now I am willing to take those actions.　　　Yes　　　No

If Yes, what will my next steps be?

____

____

____

____

If No, what keeps me in my current situation?

____

____

____

How long am I willing to remain this way?

____

____

____

____

Dealing with a change in your life is never easy. Many people interpret change as a relinquishing of control. One of most prevalent fears that humans possess is fear of loss of control. There is an underlying belief that unless you can exercise control over the future something terrible will befall you. Yet the majority of changes you experience in life are rarely under your control. Learning to walk was based upon your parents' desire for you to become more mobile and independent. Changing jobs may be the result of a company's need to downsize to survive economic challenges.

> *"The change in my job status is closely related to my family situation. After I got married, it took over four years to go through the immigration process to being with my wife and two kids. My wife is an MD, and I felt like I was rising in my career, but dealing with my wife's depression and taking care of my family obligations, including helping my parents, felt like I don't have enough time and energy to focus on my growth positively."*
> — RB

Change requires a journey from the known to the unknown, from the familiar to the unfamiliar. It's during this time that you experience transition. Transition does not always have a linear flow but is more likely to respond to the situations before us. Many of my clients express hopefulness and excitement following what they believe to be a positive interview. When they do not hear from an employer or receive a rejection letter, they can fall back into feelings of depression or apathy. We need to adapt to the ambiguities in life and accept them as part of the human condition.

When dealing with change and transition in employment, there are five elements that support success for people achieving what they want in life. They also were derived from an open-ended question posed to a group of job seekers during a panel presentation. When the group members were asked to name topics that were pertinent to their current situation and that would be helpful in finding employment, they identified five traits. These common threads show up among the hundreds of individual clients and the thousands of job seekers I have spoken to in my talks as a career counselor and coach. They are **Self-confidence, Perseverance, Acceptance, Resilience, and Commitment.**

In the following chapters, we will be examining each of these five key elements as they relate to transition as a function of change in employment.

Key Learning Points

- Change and transitions are a natural part of life.
- The world of tomorrow will look different from the world of today.
- Change and transition begin with an ending.
- Most people dedicate little of their time to planning their career paths.
- Having a plan requires a person to take responsibility for actions and choices.

What is your story around transition in general as you read through this chapter? What was it that triggered your thoughts around this?

CHAPTER TWO

Self-Confidence

"Mastering others is strength.
Mastering yourself is true power."
– Lao Tzu

Self-confidence self-assessment quiz

Mark **Yes** or **No** as it applies to your life today.

1. I awaken looking forward to the day.	Yes	No
2. I feel confident in my ability to learn to perform unfamiliar tasks.	Yes	No
3. I am open to meeting new people.	Yes	No
4. I recognize that I have unique talents that can benefit others.	Yes	No
5. I am willing to share my thoughts and feelings with others.	Yes	No
6. I am willing to try new things even if I don't fully succeed.	Yes	No
7. I rely on my own judgments and experience to make decisions.	Yes	No
8. I am aware of my negative thoughts, knowing that they don't define me.	Yes	No
9. I consider myself to be likeable.	Yes	No
10. I know when I need to ask for help.	Yes	No

To determine your score, count the number of **Yes** statements. ____

8-10 You indicate a **high** degree of ability within this area.

4-7 You indicate a **moderate** degree of ability within this area.

1-3 You indicate a **low** degree of ability within this area.

Self-confidence defined

Are people naturally self-confident, or is it more about how they build self-confidence throughout their daily lives? As a child, you were faced with the daunting task of learning to care for your needs. You moved beyond the safety of your parents' protection to interact with strangers, navigate your way into uncharted territories, and learn to set boundaries. Like most of us, you weren't completely successful the first time you tried a new behavior. Think back to the first time you attempted to ride a bicycle or drive a car. Self-confidence is a product of a sense of well-being, acceptance of body and mind, and belief in your own abilities, skills, and experience.

Oftentimes your self-confidence is affected by the feedback and input you receive from others. These are usually judgments in the form of statements from siblings, parents, and others in authority, such as teachers. Ask any four-year-old if they are able to fly to the moon or build a skyscraper and most likely you will hear a resounding, "YES!" Revisit them several years later and ask them the same questions. External influences will have shaped their new response to, "No, I couldn't do that." Perhaps they have been told they are not intelligent enough or athletic enough to continue on the path they first considered as leading to a potential career. While the words may have been intended to be thought provoking, they are often received as a harsh criticism and a predictor of future success. Because we give credence to those who we perceive as being more experienced in life, we take their comments to heart and limit opportunities that come our way.

As an undergraduate majoring in psychology at the University of Pittsburgh, I often heard references to theorist Albert Bandura and his thoughts about self-efficacy. His use of this term closely mirrors what we commonly think of as self-confidence. He viewed self-efficacy as the level of confidence you demonstrate when faced with a challenge in life. When you hold a strong sense of self-efficacy or self-confidence; you typically interpret obstacles as problem-solving opportunities. There is a stronger attachment to your areas of interest, and you're unlikely to abandon your commitment when setbacks occur. For those with a less developed sense of this trait, there is less willingness to attempt tasks that are seen outside of their ability levels and a greater focus on their failings or limitations.

While self-confidence can be affected by the words of someone in whom we place our trust, it can also come from fear of the unknown, low self-esteem, feeling unprepared, having poor time-management skills, lack of knowledge, or prior failures. Perhaps there was a time when you had a major project to complete for work and were required to do an oral presentation to your colleagues and customers. We know that speaking before a group is one of the foremost fears among people, and so there can be a tendency to avoid the experience on a conscious or unconscious level.

The time you had to spend on the assignment was competing with other priorities and each day that passed loomed over you as the deadline approached. The mind chatter begins: "Why didn't I start this sooner?" "I have so little to show that I even have a basic understanding of what I am trying to communicate." "You would have thought I would have learned to have planned better since this isn't the first time this has happened." As you stand before your audience to explain what you have done, you hope that no one sees how poor your delivery is. The ten minutes that it takes to finish feels like an eternity. You know it and so do the people listening to you. You're now setting the tone for future presentations based on the effect that this one has had on your self-confidence. This can lead to one of several options:

Option A: You can crawl back into your seat and vow to never stand in front of an audience again.

Option B: You can convince yourself that you completely lack the skills or the personality for public speaking.

Option C: You can dismiss the entire experience as being worthless to begin with.

Option D: You can learn from this experience and create a plan for being effective in future presentations.

If you chose Options A, B, or C, you're destined to remain in a holding pattern that will neither benefit you nor help build your self-confidence. If you chose Option D, it will mean that it's time to roll up your shirtsleeves and get to work on that plan. You might consider joining Toastmasters or enrolling in a public speaking class.

People vary in their degrees of self-confidence. They range from low to high and have a strong impact on accomplishing goals depending on where they are on the continuum. As a career coach, my role is to structure tasks in a way that allow the client to experience success. It may be through the assignment of writing what the client wishes to accomplish in the next five years in the various areas of their life or making a list of descriptors for the type of people with whom they enjoy working. There are no right or wrong answers, so they cannot be judged for their performance.

In the case where the client is asked to apply a new skill, such as conducting an informational interview, there is a review of the process and what is required before such a meeting is scheduled. The client is encouraged for the steps they have taken. When a task has not been completed, it becomes an opportunity to discuss what is further needed to move forward. The client may have a legitimate reason for not carrying out the task and can renegotiate it or eliminate it altogether. The reluctance to proceed may be based on the programming that the client brings to the coaching experience, which can be reframed to better serve them. Finally, there should be time to stop and feel what is involved with a new sense of self-confidence and discuss the differences compared to how they internalized similar situations in the past.

The good news is that you're not sentenced to a life fueled by negative situations and events that affect achieving what you desire in life. There are specific strategies for improving self-confidence that can be learned and incorporated into your daily routine. They will require conscious effort and may feel awkward when you first begin to apply them. There will be a tendency to revert to old behavior patterns, and having someone with whom you're accountable to help you through this can be helpful. Think about a behavior that you have considered changing. Were your successful with making that change when you attempted to do it alone? Having someone you trust in to help keep you stay focused can help assure that your goals are achieved.

Exercise: Complete each of the following statements.

One behavior that I would like to change is _________________________.

The way it currently affects my life in a negative ways is __________.

Once I had changed it, my life would be different than it is today in that I would____

Know your strengths and weaknesses

*"We deceive ourselves when we fancy that only weakness
needs support.Strength needs it far more."*
– Annie Sophie Swetchine

You can begin to build your self-confidence by focusing on your strengths and accomplishments. One exercise that is helpful in identifying accomplishments is to write five stories from your past recalling a time when you achieved a desirable result. You may have been the first in your family to graduate from college, training for and finishing a marathon, or learning to change a tire. This exercise has proven to be a springboard toward success for previous clients. As they complete their stories, we review them for themes and patterns, such as their strengths in organizing, meeting deadlines, helping others, or mastering new technology. This gives them the foundation for describing their accomplishments to others as they network and interview. A quote we often hear or see in print, "Nothing breeds success like success," has validity. When you're successful at/in something, it gives you the interest and confidence to push yourself even further or do even more to become more successful.

Knowing your strengths is important; identifying ways to compensate for the limitations you possess can be equally important. No one can do everything. One of the most frequently asked questions in an interview is, "Tell me about your weaknesses." People who are self-confident don't need to hedge on that question. One personal trait that I wrestled with when I began my career was that, in working with special needs populations, I had a tendency to internalize the work I did at a deeply personal level. The result was that I was paying a high emotional price that benefitted neither myself nor the other person. Learning to detach from the outcome after providing the best professional service possible at the time allowed me to better focus my attention while at work. If you aren't sure of what your limitations are, ask someone you trust to give you that feedback. Then actively plan for how you will address that presence in your life. You now have a valid response demonstrating how you take proactive responsibility for your limitations.

Exercise: Write about an incident in your past that affected your self-confidence. If there were a number of related incidents, focus on the earliest one you can recall. After you complete this, answer the following questions:

1. How old were you when this occurred?_______________________

2. Who was present when this occurred?_______________________

3. If there were others present, what do you recall them doing or saying in response to it?________________________________

____

____

____

4. How did you feel when this incident occurred?_____________

____

5. What belief did you create based on this incident?____________

____

6. How has this belief affected your life up to this point?_________

7. If you could create a new belief related to the incident, what would it be?____

8. How would you describe your life with this new belief in place?

____

9. On a scale of 1-10, how committed are you to incorporate this new belief into your thinking?_______________________________

10. Will you consciously begin to either write or repeat this new belief aloud to yourself at least 21 times a day for 21 continuous days? ____

Have you ever received a compliment from someone you know? It might sound something like, "You did a great job" or "Nice having you on the team." But what exactly did they mean by that? Without specifics, you have no idea what was behind their supportive words. Here is an opportunity to ask them to share what led to the compliment. "Doing a great job" could include making sure that your part of the assignment was delivered on time and covered all the salient features of the contract. It may also be based on your current client's satisfaction to the point that they recommended your business to another company. "Nice having you on the team" could mean that you keep everyone in the communication loop and are open in recognizing others for their contributions. Thank the person complimenting you immediately for their feedback and keep a journal of your interaction with them and the specific ways that you're making a difference in how the company operates. This information on how you are presenting yourself in the workplace is a valuable part of your branding. When approaching new tasks, ask yourself how you can best use the feedback from previous tasks to improve your chances for success in what you're facing now.

While it's important to be told what you're doing well, there may be times when you're told about your less than stellar performance. This can be a potential landmine for your self-confidence. Perhaps you missed a deadline or forgot to contact a client about a change in delivery date. It happens to the best of us. Rather than go on the defensive, stop, take a deep breath, and listen to what you're being told. Accept responsibility for your part in it without deflecting what occurred to another coworker or department. Make sure you're clear on what was needed and how to address it. Gather as much information as you can about the situation and use it to plan for future similar events. If needed, schedule a time to meet with others who were affected to make sure that they understand what they can expect from you.

Exercise:

Part A: Make a list of your top five strengths. For each of them write a story about the time when you used this in your life and how you benefitted from it. Be sure to include the feelings that you experienced as you tapped into your strength. After you finish each of your stories, answer the following questions:

1. What strength did I describe?_______________________________________

2. What was I doing to demonstrate this strength?_________________________

3. If I was not doing this in isolation, who was around me at the time?

____

4. What emotions did I experience as I demonstrated this strength?

____

5. What were two other occasions when I used this strength? What were the results of using it?___________________________________

6. How am I using this strength today?___________________________

Part B: Now make a list of three weaknesses or limitations you identify in your life. For each of them write a story about your earliest recollection of them as best you can. Be sure to include the feelings that you experienced as part of this event. After you finish each of your stories, answer the following questions:

What weakness or limitation did I describe?___________________________

What was I doing at the time I first recognized it?___________________

If I was not doing this in isolation, who was around me at the time?

____

What did I say to myself or hear others say to me at the time?

____

What emotions did I experience at this time?___________________

What were two other occasions since then that I reminded myself of this weakness or limitation?___________________________

How does its presence affect me today in being successful?

____

What can I do to change it?___________________________________

How will my life look and feel different when I make this change?

Affirmation:

I make acknowledge my strengths and aspirations, and view my weaknesses as opportunities for growth and self-improvement.

Think positively

*"Man often becomes what he believes himself to be.
If I keep on saying to myself that I cannot do a certain
thing, it is possible that I may end by really becoming
incapable of doing it. On the contrary, if I have the belief
that I can do it, I shall surely acquire the capacity to do it
even if I may not have it at the beginning."*
– Mahatma Gandhi

Think of the power of words and thoughts. We are reminded of the eloquent speeches of leaders, philosophers, and orators and their ability to survive through the centuries. Our words describe our past, proclaim our present, and shape our future. Two of the most powerful words in the English language are, "I am…" What follows defines how we see ourselves and how we project that image into the world. "I am intelligent." "I am athletic." "I am considerate of others." These positive attributes seek fertile ground for opportunities to further growth and development. At the same time statements such as "I am a loser," "I am too old to be hired," and " I am too set in my ways," will also demonstrate their power in the way our life plays itself out.

> *"[Regarding the loss of my job I felt] surprise and*
> *then determination to achieve a successful outcome."*
> — BJ

How do you typically finish your "I am..." declarations? Are they positive in nature, or are they peppered with negative judgments? An easy way to identify the impact that your beliefs of who you are have on how you present yourself to others, is to stand before a full-length mirror and state your "I ams" aloud. Observe how your body reflects the words you utter. If you truly believe what you say, your facial expressions and physical posture will match those assertions, whether they are positive or negative. Ask yourself which of these messages you plan to take into your next interview. This is what is commonly referred to as "self-fulfilling prophecy," in which your current self-perception influences future results. If you wish to boost your self-confidence, practice making a positive declaration beginning with "I am" three times a day with no less than seven repetitions. Do this while placing your hands on your hips with legs spread apart and head held erect. Locate where you feel your self-confidence in your body. You will use this later to determine its presence in situations that call for it. Watch for others who you see as having self-confidence, and observe how they carry themselves and how they use their words and body language to convey their inner beliefs. When you first begin this exercise you may admonish yourself by saying, "Who are you kidding? You don't really believe this about yourself." Or "Aren't you full of yourself. No one likes a braggart." This is the side of you that will keep you safe but stagnant. Being humble is about accepting who you are and what you have to offer and then quietly and confidently sharing that with the world.

> *"[It helps] believing that there is a quality*
> *job match out there. I just have to find it."*
> – GW

Exercise: Complete each of the following statements beginning with "I am." Just write the first word that comes to mind.

I am ____________________________________.

I am ____________________________________.

I am ____________________________________.

I am ____________________________________.

I am ____________________________________.

Now look over them and decide if any of them are negative. This will provide you with a sense of whether you see yourself in a positive or negative light based on their frequency. Ask yourself what you would like in their place and write a new statement in the positive.

I am ____________________________________.

I am ____________________________________.

I am ____________________________________.

I am ____________________________________.

I am ____________________________________.

Stand in front of a mirror and repeat each of the positive statements aloud, and listen to what your mind tells you. How do you feel as you hear your words?

Now choose one of the five statements to focus on for the next thirty days. If you hear a negative message as you speak, say, "STOP." Then continue to repeat your statement ten times. Do this three times a day until it becomes embedded in your neural pathways. If you miss a day, you will need to start over the next day. As you repeat your statement, be conscious of your words so that you're not doing it mechanically. The more energy and emotion you infuse into it, the more powerful it will become. Once it has become a part of you, choose another statement and repeat the process.

> *"I just need to remember to look forward and find what is good for me...despite the fact that it is truly better that I am no longer at the company."*
> – GW

Affirmation:

I maintain a positive mindset allowing me to attract the perfect career opportunity that aligns with my skills and aspirations.

Build physical strength and stamina

"In order for man to succeed in life, God provided him with two means, education and physical activity. Not separately, one for the soul and the other for the body, but for the two together.With these means, man can attain perfection."
– Plato

As you think about self-confidence, consider the role that good health has on your ability to reach your goals, face the challenges that life presents, and take on new tasks. There is a definite correlation between your physical health and your mental functioning. Recall a time when you had a cold or the flu. The last thing you felt like doing was sitting in a meeting having to focus your attention on what was being said or trying to map out a sales strategy. Your body just wants to recuperate and not expend energy on major thought processes. So what does it take to minimize the time you spend lying in bed coughing and rushing off to the bathroom?

Maintaining good health requires that you eat a balanced diet, exercise regularly, and get the proper amount of rest. Right now there are so many recommended approaches to eating properly, and I am not here as a proponent of one over the other. Most likely by the time you read this book, there will be at least four new diets guaranteed to keep you healthy. Find a plan that works for you and your lifestyle. I would suggest that you limit your intake of sugar and caffeine based on their effects on your body. You want to regulate your metabolism more evenly as opposed to the spikes that a morning dose of donuts and coffee creates in your system.

Exercise: Think about your options for exercising. What is motivating for some may be drudgery for others. Now consider the ones that work for you.

Types of exercise I prefer:	
Frequency of each exercise:	
How I feel after exercising:	
Exercise:	Feeling(s):

When it comes to exercise, it's important that you identify a routine that fits into your schedule and keeps you motivated. You may enjoy hiking, swimming, team sports, or dancing. The list is endless. Whatever you choose, make sure that it builds strength and stamina. This is what you will need to keep pace in the workplace. You know you're on the right track when you begin to sweat and your heart rate increases during your physical activities. Remember that exercising provides oxygen and nutrients to the brain which can actually make you smarter when it comes to understanding and completing the task before you.

I remember pulling what we called "all-nighters" when I was in college. Back then I would be sitting at a typewriter (pre-PC) and writing a term paper until the wee hours of the morning. Then I would drag myself off to class with little chance of catching a nap. String two or three such days together and you have the making of a physical collapse. My resistance would be negligible, and I was a prime candidate for catching any bug that was in the air.

Being deficient in any of these three areas could easily impact your self-confidence. When we are carrying those extra pounds it affects how our clothing fits, how we carry ourselves when we walk, and our energy levels. Exercising not only makes you stronger, it gives you a sense of accomplishment as you lengthen your time walking, swim more laps, or burn those excess calories. Getting the right amount of sleep helps you stay alert and focused during the day. All of these also contribute to reducing your stress levels, allowing you to better handle the challenges of the day.

> *"[What helps during this time is] exercising*
> *every morning at the gym."*
> — MB, Sales

Affirmation:

As my physical strength and stamina increase, so does my confidence, increasing my capacity to tackle any task that comes my way.

Practice modesty and humility

> *"Knowledge is as infinite as the universe.*
> *The man who claims to know all only reveals to*
> *all that he really knows nothing."*
> — Suzy Kassem

Humility is often confused with active denial of who you are and the talents you possess. Modesty and humility encompass a secure understanding of your talents and the non-egocentric use of them. If you're articulate, you can use that ability to express your words in a manner that motivates and elevates others. If you're analytical, you can use that ability to drill deeply into a problem to identify solutions that will benefit others. You acknowledge your contributions without needing to direct everyone's attention to them as a way of increasing your self-importance. When you misuse your gift of articulation it can show up as sarcasm or put-downs. When you misuse your gift of analysis it can become disparaging and overbearing. There can be a fine line between expressing your knowledge of a particular area and crossing over into arrogance. Think of your skills and talents and ask others close to you how they perceive you using them. It's helpful to work with the feedback they provide.

Slipping into arrogance can be subtle and seductive when your self-confidence is questionable. There is a tendency to elevate your own self-worth at the expense of others. You may know at least one person who parades their expertise and intellect before everyone they know. They generate an air of superiority that makes them difficult to be around. This is different from the person who communicates their intelligence without attaching self-importance to it. Arrogance carries with it the denial of what others may have to contribute to solving a problem. There is only one point of view that matters—theirs. In this case, it's natural to withdraw knowing that any attempt to have the other person listen is futile. There is little likelihood that the behaviors surrounding their arrogance will change since it serves a need within them. They seek out opportunities to exercise their arrogance, creating a self-image that thrives on situations that place them above others in their minds. In doing so, they forfeit respect, acceptance, and love from others.

So how would a confident person deal with others sharing their ideas? Be open to what others have to say. Sometimes even the most outlandish thoughts bear some kernels of truth that could lead to a solution. This is the time to suspend judgment over the rational and just listen. Invite the other person to share what is behind their thinking. They may only need more time to think it through. Don't always expect that people will have all the answers at once. You can always end the discussion with, "Why don't you think about that and I'll get back to you." Make sure that you do make a point of reconnecting with them so that this does not become a statement of dismissal of their ideas. Give it the attention it deserves before your next conversation.

You can learn so much when you listen to the experiences of others, even if you don't always immediately agree with them. If you begin to sense arrogance creeping up on you, ask yourself what is going on with your own thinking. Oftentimes you will find that you're feeling threatened in some way and your arrogance is a way of shutting that out. It's important to root out the source of that threat and decide what you want to do about it.

People who are self-confident and humble have no trouble giving others credit for their work. It's tempting to accept praise for a job well done and claim total responsibility for the accomplishment. That works well when you're accountable for 100% of the task. What happens when you are dependent on others to ensure that the work meets acceptable standards and is delivered on time? This is an opportunity to point out the contributions made by others while still leaving room for your own role in the success of the project. There is nothing wrong with saying, "The job would never have come in under budget if it hadn't been for Jane's analysis of the costs involved" or "Bob volunteered to stay late several times to participate in meetings to assess our progress and provided some excellent suggestions that helped move the team forward." What you do for others will hopefully be returned in kind. It also demonstrates that you're secure enough to share what others have done.

How did you feel when you were not acknowledged for your efforts in the group meeting its goals? Do you feel slighted and unappreciated? Would you feel motivated to contribute to the team during upcoming projects or would you have a tendency to hold back, wondering if others valued what you had to offer? Those left outside the circle of success may think, "Why bother?" or "Does anyone really care if I show up or not?" When you overlook giving recognition to others, the damage that can be done could have lasting effects on the solidarity of the team. When you recognize the part that each individual played in achieving success, you build camaraderie and dedication to maintaining a higher standard of performance. Your co-workers will seek you out as the one they want to have working next to them.

Remember a time when you were introduced to a task that required you to apply skills in a way you hadn't done before. Perhaps a new product line was being introduced and you weren't quite sure how to pitch it. Or the company was now using a new system to track its shipments. Mastering the task came second nature to you, but not so easy to those around you. You could either stand by and watch them struggle to figure it out on their own or you could serve as a teacher to explain just how it works.

I remember the time I spent my day off meeting with a co-worker to explain a concept she had been struggling with that I had no trouble comprehending. After learning where she was having difficulty, I broke the concept down into manageable pieces and guided her through the process of putting her ideas onto paper.

After several hours of working together, she announced, "You mean it's that simple?" She now felt confident that she could carry the task out on her own and her subsequent performance proved that to be true. When you take time to help others it helps build a bond between you. From that day on I felt a positive shift in our relationship. This is how win-win outcomes result.

Exercise: Make a list of your natural talents. These are skills and abilities that you possess that are effortless for you to perform. Choose the top five and rank them in the chart below. Next to each one write at least one example of how you use it in your life. Now think of how you could share that with others as a way of instructing them in the skill

Natural talent	Examples of how I use it	How I could share it with others

Natural talent	Examples of how I use it	How I could share it with others

Affirmation:

I embrace the virtues of modesty and humility as a job seeker, knowing that they are an accumulation of the collective efforts, guidance, and opportunities presented to me throughout my life.

Express gratitude

*"Do not spoil what you have by desiring what
you have not; remember that what you now have was
once among the things you only hoped for."*
– Epicurus

One of the choices you have is to decide whether you will focus on what you have or what you lack. Try this: Think of something that you believe you're missing in life right now. It may be a job, a relationship, or a hefty bank account. Now think about something that you do have in your life that elicits joy and a sense of well-being related to the people, things, and circumstances present. Perhaps it's having a friend to confide in, your good health, or a trip you've been planning for years. What just happened to your thoughts about lack? Most of you will find that you cannot hold two such thoughts simultaneously. The more you practice gratitude for what you have, the more you find it to be the mainstay of who you are.

Exercise: We are often reminded of the importance of expressing our gratitude to others for what they have done to help us along the way. There are times when we would benefit from reaching out to those individuals in gratitude, for it's in giving that we receive.

In **Column A** list ten people from your past who have aided you in some way. They may be living or deceased. In **Column B** write what it was that each of them did specifically that affected you. In **Column C** indicate how you wish to express your gratitude. It may be face to face, through a card or email, by telephone, or in any other manner you can think of. In **Column D** write the date by which you commit to doing this. Finally, in **Column E** place a checkmark across from the name when you have sent your message of gratitude. If the person is deceased, read the message of gratitude and perform a ritual around it such as burning it or putting it in the mail with only their first name on it.

Column A	Column B	Column C	Column D	Column E
Name of Person	What He or She Did	How to Thank	Date to Thank	✓ When Done

Being grateful for what you have allows you to be open to possibilities and opportunities. Your mind opens to availability rather than scarcity and limitation. Like I once was, you may have found it difficult to find much to be grateful for. People I would meet would often tell me that I was my own worst enemy. I was so caught up in my own feelings of lack that I couldn't fathom what they were saying. Rather than feeling like King Midas, whose touch turned everything around him to gold, mine felt more like it was turning everything into lead. At one point I hit such a low point that there was no other way to go but up. Knowing that I must do something to turn my life around, I began to devote my time to learning how to alter my negative thinking.

One technique to practice is to keep a gratitude list. Each night before going to bed, write down at least five specific areas of your life for which you're grateful. It may not be easy at first, but the more you develop this habit, the more natural it will become for you. My perspective on life began to change when new options appeared after using this practice. One of them involved a chance to move across the country for a new position. I had never traveled much beyond a 100-mile radius from where I was born, and now I was looking at driving to the other side of the country with nothing more than a map and a destination. The trip became an adventure as I observed the changes in landscape passing from one state to another and figured out how to deal with a damaged tire and an overheated engine along the way. These were minor incidents when I think about what I learned about myself and my self-determination.

Not only can you feel grateful for what you have today, you can also frame what is missing in your life in a new light. Was there a time that you wanted more than ever to be in a relationship? Did you approach meeting someone as the answer to your prayers until you realized that it was not going to be permanent? If you make a conscious decision to enjoy your single life and what it has to offer, you may adopt an entirely new perspective on life. You have the freedom to do what you want, when you want, with whomever you want. Focus on what your friendships give you in meeting your needs. As you accept that, think about what lessons you learned as a single person. In doing so, the condition could change. It did for me. Now I'm grateful for all that I'm learning within a committed relationship. The same can be true when applied to work or any other condition you're dealing with.

Exercise: It's easy enough to express our gratitude toward those with whom we feel an affinity. But what about those people and institutions that we believe may have done us an injustice in life? Perhaps their actions resulted in some loss, such as the end of a relationship, a job, or your finances. To move forward with your life it's necessary to release the bond between you, especially if it's one-sided on your part. Rather than interpret what happened as an affront to you, how can you see it as a gift? If you were terminated from your position at work, what did you learn from the experience? Perhaps it provided clarity in seeking out future employment leading to the work you love to do today.

In the exercise below, in **Column A** write the name of the person or organization that you may be holding on to with resentment. In **Column B** write the nature of the transgression. In **Column C** write the gift you received from it. Now thank the person or organization mentally. If you have truly let go, you will feel a sense of relief and lightness following the exercise.

Column A	Column B	Column C
Name of Person or Organization	**Nature of Perceived Transgression**	**The Gift I Received from It**
Ken Smith	*Recommended a demotion for me*	*Motivated me to seek other employment leading to a career change*

Affirmation:

I express gratitude for the opportunities that come my way, finding joy in the small victories and progress I achieve every day.

Foster confidence-building behaviors

"My belief is that during conversations,
it's not so much what you say;
it's how you say it that matters.
What's being heard is secondary to what's being seen,
as body language leads the discussion and
dictates the mood."
– Jarod Kintz

Identify someone you know who you consider to be the poster child for confidence. What is their posture like as they enter a room? Do they walk in with their heads held high, shoulders squared, sure-footed? Is there a smile on their face? Are they making eye contact with people as they greet them? These are all learned behaviors. Some people are more adept at demonstrating them than others. Here are some tips for communicating self-confidence through your body language:

Think of the messages that your **facial expressions** send to others. There are times when you're consciously aware of the expressions on your face and other times when the signals are unconsciously transmitted. This is what is registering with the listener, and he or she is making decisions and judgments based on these impressions. The next time you're engaged in conversation, be aware of the differences between what is being communicated through the upper half and the lower half of the speaker's face.

You will notice that more information is conveyed through the upper half.

We talk about the **eyes** being the "windows of the soul." That statement comes from the power of the messages transmitted in and around your eyes. In Western culture, we learn to maintain eye contact while speaking. Maintaining eye contact for too long a period will likely create discomfort for the listener. At the same time, constantly breaking eye contact may be interpreted as an attempt to withhold information. We typically break eye gaze every 5 to 15 seconds. The role of the listener is to focus on the speaker during the conversation. When the listener turns his eyes away from the speaker, it's often interpreted as boredom or disinterest.

The **eyebrows** also communicate a variety of intentions. This includes disapproval, disagreement, and disbelief as well as their counterparts. Your words may be communicating one message while your eyebrows are transmitting something very different. Which do you think is more indicative of that the speaker is thinking or feeling? Be aware of your own tendencies to send incongruent signals with your eyebrows. One way to check such incongruence is to have someone record you as you share information and analyze your facial responses.

Confident people **smile** in a natural way. They don't paste on a grin that stretches from ear to ear but smile when they connect with the words of the person to whom they are speaking. In doing so they create a comfort level. Just as raised eyebrows can transmit a message of disbelief, a forced smile can convey smugness, arrogance, or avoidance. It may also reflect an extreme discomfort with what is being discussed.

Be aware of what your **posture** and **body stance** communicate. When speaking to another person, make sure that your legs are aligned with your shoulders. Your feet should be planted firmly, 4-6 inches apart, with your weight evenly distributed on both legs. Position your shoulders so that they are back, but not to the point where you appear to have a board pasted to your back. There should be a slight tilt to your body so you do not come across as aggressive. Experiment with positioning your arms and hands so that they look natural and comfortable. Folding your arms across your chest can be interpreted as defensiveness, and placing your hands in your pockets can be seen as discomfort or an attempt to withhold information.

You want to feel your back resting against the back of the chair with your shoulders rolled slightly forward. If you feel yourself beginning to slouch, reposition yourself without calling attention to the shift in your position.

When seated, think about the positioning of your **legs and feet**. Keep both feet on the floor. Try not to cross your legs, which can be distracting to the other person. It also decreases circulation because it places pressure on your veins.

If you're a person who tends to communicate with **hand gestures**, it's important to keep them in check. Have you ever observed a person who used exaggerated hand motions to the point where you became so mesmerized by their hands that you lost track of the message? Are there times when using a grand gesture would be appropriate in demonstrating a point, especially if you're not prone to using them? Avoid the gesture of pointing, particularly if you're standing close to the other person. Pointing carries a negative connotation of intimidation and aggression. If you need to point, do so with an open palm. If you tend to be a pen clicker or a table tapper, find a less intrusive way to occupy your hands. These behaviors may be seen as indicative of nervousness, boredom, or inattention.

Be aware that there are cultural differences that accompany communication. If you're in a situation that involves people from cross-cultural backgrounds, familiarize yourself with their styles of communication.

Given these suggestions for how to communicate with confidence, how would you rate yourself on your current ability to do so effectively? Is there room for improvement? As humans it's important to accept that we will never communicate perfectly, but we can fine-tune our skills in this area.

If you find your self-talk around this to be, "But I could never do that," you have already lost the battle. Accept the fact that you may feel uncomfortable with these new behaviors at first, but with practice, they will become more natural for you as time passes. Since these are observable behaviors, enlist the help of a friend or coach to provide feedback on your progress before you go public with it. Then have your partner present as you walk into a roomful of people to mentally note how you're doing. Remember that it doesn't have to be perfect the first time you attempt this. You can refine your behavior based on their feedback. Think of your poster child and how he or she would look, and imagine yourself to be like him/her if that helps reduce your anxiety.

Exercise: In the chart below, write the behavior you wish to emulate. It may be making appropriate eye contact or tracking a conversation through non-verbals, such as nodding. Now name one person you know who demonstrates that behavior. Next, choose to commit to developing that behavior over the next month using that person as a model. For that month, imagine yourself being that person demonstrating that behavior, consciously practicing that behavior consistently for one month. It's important to emulate an action every day. You may find it helpful to keep notes on your experience with this behavior.

Name of Person whose behavior(s) you want to emulate:		
Behavior(s) to emulate	**Dates**	**Notes on my experience**
	1	
	2	
	3	
	4	
	5	
	6	
	7	
	8	
	9	
	10	
	11	
	12	
	13	
	14	
	15	
	16	
	17	

Name of Person whose behavior(s) you want to emulate:		
Behavior(s) to emulate	Dates	Notes on my experience
	18	
	19	
	20	
	21	
	22	
	23	
	24	
	25	
	26	
	27	
	28	
	29	
	30	
	31	

Affirmation:

I embrace confidence-building behaviors during my job search, knowing that confidence is the magnet that attracts success to me.

Continue to learn

"Always desire to learn something useful."
– Sophocles

Using what you have learned from your planning exercises, think of a skill that you currently lack or one that improving upon could benefit you. How would adding this to your repertoire increase your employability and self-confidence? There are several key areas that need updating throughout your career. They include communication, problem solving, and technology. It's critical to have a plan for staying current, especially when you consider the changes that have occurred in this decade alone. Imagine sitting in an interview and being asked questions about the technical advancements in your field and realizing that you have been depending on antiquated methods that can keep you out of the running. How confident will you look or be when you stare back at the interviewer clueless as to the latest tools and trends?

Take advantage of the learning opportunities available to you. There are countless numbers of free and low-cost webinars on every imaginable topic. Once you have registered for one of them, you will receive notifications of future events on similar topics. In many cases, they are available as recordings for a limited period so you needn't worry

"After almost 12 years of putting myself last, I finally took a class I have been wanting to take for more than ten years but couldn't due to my fulltime job."
– EY, Graphic artist

about being present in real time. Keep track of the webinar titles, dates, and content to demonstrate to others how you're staying current. There are also numerous "how-to" videos online, such as YouTube, as well as tutorials.

Set aside a specific amount of time each day to dedicate yourself to such learning. There are also online training programs leading to certifications in a variety of areas. When I was transitioning from working in the schools to career coaching, I sought out certification programs that could be completed based on my schedule as opposed to waiting for a weekly class over four to six months. I was thus able to finish a certification well in advance of the allotted time. Find a program that works for you. If you benefit from a traditional classroom environment, by all means sign up for classes at a local college or through community-based programs. Always keep your final goal in mind and ask yourself how this particular learning experience will support you achieving it.

> *"[It has been helpful to be] taking art classes, completing my certificate, taking classes in my computer programs."*
> — SB, Retail cashier

There is great value in joining interest groups related to your focus areas. These groups exist as online virtual groups, face-to-face gatherings, or a combination of both. One of the first things I did when I was considering a new career direction was to find the names and locations of such groups and attend the next meeting they were having. Commit to attending two or three before deciding if this particular group is right for you. You may discover that their presentation style aligns with how you choose to learn and interact. The longer you stay with a group, the more comfortable you will become with the content and you will begin to share your background with it. If you're in the process of moving to a new field, you will begin to become accustomed to the language and jargon that is spoken among the group. If you're so inclined, you may be motivated to take on a leadership or service role to accelerate the process. Once you begin to identify with a specific group, you move from the outside to the inside of the circle.

Exercise:

Part A: In **Column A** identify five skills that you would like to learn or improve related to either your current or anticipated job duties. In **Column B** write why it's important for you to obtain them. **In Column C** identify your means for learning them. It could be by attending class on a brick and mortar campus, online, a combination of both, books and manuals, or asking someone to teach you directly. If another resource comes up for you, include it. In **Column D** write the date by which you will complete mastery of the skill. Being exposed to a skill is not the same as being able to apply it in your work.

Column A Skill	Column B Why you want to learn it	Column C Means for learning it	Column D Date of Mastery

Column A Skill	Column B Why you want to learn it	Column C Means for learning it	Column D Date of Mastery

Part B: In **Column A** write five areas of information that you would like to know more about to be better at what you do. In **Column B** write two reasons for being knowledgeable in each area you identified. In **Column C** list your resources for gathering this knowledge. It may be specific books and journals, online articles, classes, lectures, webinars, etc. In **Column D** write the date accompanying the completion of each of your resources.

Column A Area of information	Column B Why you want to learn it	Column C Resources	Column D Date of completion

Column A Area of information	Column B Why you want to learn it	Column C Resources	Column D Date of completion

Affirmation:

I embrace a mindset of continuous learning during my job search, allowing me to expand my knowledge, skills, and expertise.

Develop an action plan

"By failing to prepare, you are preparing to fail."
– Benjamin Franklin

Planning is the roadmap we create to help us in reaching our destination. Planning involves considering various outcomes and identifying ways for approaching them. Think of how you would plan a road trip across the country. You have a set starting and ending point as well as an arrival time. Halfway through your trip, you encounter major road construction resulting from a landslide that occurred an hour before you reached that section of the highway. Without an alternate plan, you would be stranded there for hours and time is of the essence. What would your alternate plans be? Would you act impulsively or spend time weighing your options before taking action? There are those individuals who believe that doing something or anything when confronted by a challenging situation is the most effective approach to take. They deal with the consequences later (or sometimes sooner).

*"After [the] loss of a job I held for 11 years,
I think I pretended that "it was meant to be," but in
hindsight I know there were things I could have done
better, like starting job training when I could see that
the ship was about to sink. I had a lot of resentment that I
had not been appreciated or rewarded suitably,
and the end of the job was a kind of a relief."*
— EY, Graphic designer

Then there are those who see life as a series of actions taken following a trial and error approach. Just pick any road and see where it takes you. If it doesn't turn out to be what you had hoped for, choose another road, ad infinitum. There is little time spent thinking about consequences since that is time taken away from heading down the next road. It makes for a great adventure with no clear end in mind.

If you have pursued either of these two previous plans and found them to be less than desirable, there is another option available. It involves conscious planning to achieve your goals and reach your destination. While it tends to be linear in direction, it allows for the unexpected. This is typically what we refer to as having a Plan A and a Plan B. Most people stop at Plan A. Along with planning comes the necessary preparation to ensure that you have the right equipment for the task. Think what your experience would be like if you packed all of your diving equipment for a trip to the mountains. Sounds rather elementary, but it's what people often do on a metaphorical level when they set out on their career path.

As a career development specialist working with high school students with special needs, one of my roles was to assemble teams consisting of various constituents including the student, family members, educators, and outside agencies whose purpose was to create a transition plan. The team was assembled in the student's freshman year and tracked until graduation. The student was the center of attention regardless of ability level. We addressed nine life areas including career, health needs, and living arrangements. In many cases, it was the first time that parents were truly listening to their son's or daughter's thoughts about their future. Imagine nine blank sheets being filled with actions that would be taken prior to our next meeting.

Once those actions had been listed, the next step was to identify the person(s) who would be involved in its completion with a target date for accountability. Everyone present was expected to sign off on the plan and their commitment to doing their part. This was the student's road map to their future. Each subsequent year we would revisit the plan to ascertain what was still in the plan and what new information or experience caused an adjustment to be made. While the meetings were scheduled to last two hours, the general consensus was that participants could not believe how quickly the time passed. This was largely due to the value they saw in the process. Years later I had the privilege of learning how this action plan led to the quality of life the student was experiencing as an adult as I reconnected with students on social media.

In my current work with clients, it's imperative that each person leaves a session with a set of action items to complete. Each action item is designed to address a specific need or concern. Since no two clients have the same exact goals, their assignments may differ vastly. One client may be needing to research a specific training program while another client may be scheduling appointments to gather information about a new career path being considered. These items help to keep the client focused and on task. They also serve as benchmarks for progress in the process. The next coaching session usually begins with a review of the action items and what the client has learned from them.

One of your steps toward being hired is participating in the interview process. This is one situation that definitely calls for planning and preparation to be considered as a serious contender. My own early days of interviewing are a clear reminder of how the process has evolved over time. Initially, all that was required was the ability to respond in a coherent manner demonstrating that there was some understanding of the job opening. Because there was a plethora of job openings in my field, it didn't take much to receive a job offer. Using the same strategy today would not likely ensure that the applicant make it through the first round of interviews. Today's job market requires you to conduct thorough research on the company and rehearse potential questions and scenarios. If you don't, the next applicant will.

When doing your research find out what the biggest challenges of the company are. Then identify ways that you can contribute to being part of the solution. What skills and experiences do you possess that can turn their problems around? Consider this information as you craft your resume and rehearse your interview responses. In most cases, job seekers focus on their needs as opposed to what their employers are looking for to meet theirs.

Your planning should include creating a chart that lists your research results with company needs, followed by your specific skills and experiences that apply. A third column should contain strategies for how you would approach such problems based on what you have found to be successful. The earlier in your career that you begin to gather such data, the stronger you will be in being perceived as the "go-to" person for solutions. This is a function of knowing who you are and what you have to offer. Think of the effect that this will have on your self-confidence as you refer to your proven track record of accomplishments.

Company needs	My related skills and experience	Strategies for addressing need
Lack of cooperation between departments in meeting established deadlines	Consistent ability to meet deadlines Team building Active listening skills	Begin with one-on-one meetings to identify problem areas Elicit potential solutions from each person interviewed Meet with individual departments for a SWOT analysis Conduct a strategic planning meeting to include potential solutions from individual departments

You can overwhelm yourself during the planning process by taking on too much at one time. Consider the end result and then begin to break it down into smaller achievable steps. Some people prefer to "begin with the end in mind" and work backward while others like to begin with the first step based on where they are today. The strategy depends on how you plan and what motivates you to continue your progress toward your goal. The psychology behind this is what is referred to as successive approximation, in which each action takes you one step closer to your final goal. Even clients with low levels of self-confidence when we initially begin our work are capable of action in small increments. Write your planning process below:

Company needs	My related skills and experience	Strategies for addressing need

Even if you're not working with a career professional, consider taking the time to outline the steps needed to achieve your goals. Then identify specific times when you will be reviewing them. Decide if there are any adjustments that need to be made and commit them to paper. Ask yourself how they relate to your final goal and determine if this is still your final destination. If it's not, what does your new one look like? The path to success may require you to seriously reconsider the steps needed to reach it. You may also find that new circumstances can affect your plans. Perhaps a new business opportunity becomes available, you marry and decide to relocate to another part of the country to be closer to your spouse's family, or you decide that the work you're currently doing is no longer satisfying. Now what? What part of your plan needs revision and where will it take you?

Exercise: This exercise is an opportunity to begin planning for your future rather than leaving it open to chance. It's your starting point, knowing that it will be subject to change based on new circumstances and information. Commit to identifying a scheduled time for reviewing your plan and making the necessary corrections. You may create a separate plan for the goals you have set in each of your life areas.

Today's date _______________________ Life Area _________________

Goal ____

Action steps for achieving my goal:

1. ____

   ____

2. ____

   ____

3. ____

   ____

4. ____

   ____

5. ____

____

Date of next review: ______________________________

Affirmation:

I am committed to developing a strategic action plan during my job search, outlining the specific actions I need to take to achieve the goals I create.

Gain experience

"Experience tells you what to do;
confidence allows you to do it."
– Stan Smith

We know that there are 86,400 seconds in a 24-hour day. If you were to have one experience every ten seconds, that would be over eight thousand experiences per day. Of course, that depends on how one

"Setting small goals daily."
– AL

would define an experience. If you consider an experience to be a personal encounter with some aspect of the environment, this might not be an overestimation. It could be as simple as swerving to avoid a collision with an oncoming vehicle (less than ten seconds of reaction time for that experience) or translate to a more complex interpretation based on a collection of numerous discrete experiences (hours or days to scale a mountain). Many experiences will go unnoticed, such as driving a familiar route or performing a similar rote task. You may be more likely to notice experiences that are novel because they require a more cognitive conscious focus. It's these experiences that are filed away for future reference as they hold a more prominent place in our memories.

Exercise: Part A: Make a list of successful tasks you have performed in life. Refrain from making judgments as to how important they were. All that matters is that you completed the task. The longer the list the better. Next to each task describe what you did to prepare for it and what you did along the way to achieve it. For example, you may have had a major exam that you needed to pass in a specific subject. To prepare for it you read the assigned chapter prior to the class, you paid attention to the material as the teacher presented it, you took notes during the class, and you set aside the time needed to study. When it was time to take the exam, you focused your attention on the test in front of you, you read each question carefully, and you paced yourself so that you would answer all of the questions. If there was a question you were unsure of, you moved on to the next one, giving yourself enough time to return to it. When you had completed all of the questions to the best of your ability, you congratulated yourself on a job well done. All that remained to do was to wait for the results.

Successful tasks	What I did to prepare for them	What I did to achieve it

Successful tasks	What I did to prepare for them	What I did to achieve it

This exercise can be applied to any task. It could be painting your living room, planting a vegetable garden, changing the oil in your car, or selling raffle tickets.

Part B: Now think about what you would be doing in your current or future job. What tasks are included? Using the same technique from above, write down what you would do to prepare for it and what steps you would take along the way to ensure its successful completion.

Successful tasks	What I will do to prepare for them	What I will do to achieve it

This is your game plan for success. You're tapping into your successes from the past to improve the likelihood of your success in the future. Is it a guarantee that you will reach your target with 100% accuracy? If you manage to do that, great. But even if you don't, you can incorporate what you learned in the process. Remember that every experience has value to it. It's up to you to identify what that is.

One way to improve your chances of successfully completing a task is to break it down into a small achievable goal. You may have heard of SMART goals. These are goals that are Specific, Measurable, Attainable, Realistic, and Timed. Let's analyze a common goal that people set as a New Year's resolution. They share with their friends that they want to lose weight. That's a rather broad statement that can be difficult to assess when it comes to being successful.

> *"Be disciplined about goals and set realistic [ones].*
> *Celebrate and acknowledge what is good."*
> *-JB, Administrative professional*

Now let's apply the five components of a SMART goal and see what the difference would be.

Specific: To drop 10 pounds

Measurable: Going from 170 to 160 pounds

Attainable: There are no physical conditions that I have that would prevent me from achieving that goal.

Realistic: 10 pounds is doable if I pace myself, incorporating both dietary and exercise changes into my daily routine

Timed: In a two-month period, starting tomorrow

For a career-related goal, you may create the following:

Specific: To complete my master's degree in engineering

Measurable: There will be a given number of courses to enroll in and pass **A**ttainable: The program allows me to extend my classes over a three-year period, and I can take many of them online

Realistic: This is doable if I pace myself by taking 15 credits annually

Timed: I earn my degree in three years

You may also think about setting goals to be promoted within a company, obtain a new skill, start your own business, or write a book.

Exercise: Goal setting. Use the information you have just read to create a list of goals upon which to focus over the next few weeks or months. Refer to them on a daily basis to track your progress on each of them.

Goal:

Specific:

Measurable:

Attainable:

Realistic:

Timed:

Goal:

Specific:

Measurable:

Attainable:

Realistic:

Timed:

Goal:

Specific:

Measurable:

Attainable:

Realistic:

Timed:

Goal:

Specific:

Measurable:

Attainable:

Realistic:

Timed:

<table>
<tr><td>

Goal:

Specific:

Measurable:

Attainable:

Realistic:

Timed:

</td></tr>
</table>

<table>
<tr><td>

Goal:

Specific:

Measurable:

Attainable:

Realistic:

Timed:

</td></tr>
</table>

Now you have a way to objectively measure your progress toward achieving your goal. As you create your SMART goals, you will notice that they may generate others that support a main goal. For example, when you look at the Attainable component related to losing weight, you see that both dietary and exercise changes are called for. You now have the basis for creating two additional SMART goals to support your weight loss. They will require that you evaluate your current eating habits and adjust them to reduce the number of calories you consume each day as well as planning an exercise program to burn the calories you take in.

Affirmation:

I recognize that each experience contributes to my growth and enhances my professional journey.

Surround yourself with confident people

*"Your circle of friends must match your
own aspirations and dreams, or you will find
little support when you need it most."*
– Leon Brown

Keep away from people who try to belittle your ambitions. Small people often do that, but the really great make you feel that you, too, can become great. When you're seeking to bring big plans to fruition, it's important with whom you regularly associate. Hang out with friends who are like-minded and who are also designing purpose-filled lives. Similarly, be that kind of friend for your friends.

One way to establish a reference point for where you are in your life is to look at the people with whom you spend significant time. We tend to seek out those who share our beliefs and values. Before you can do that you need to be clear on what those beliefs and values are for you.

Exercise A: On the following page, make a list of statements beginning with the words, "I believe." You may write, "I believe in the innate goodness of people" or "I believe that people can't be trusted." This is an opportunity to be totally honest with yourself as to how you see the world. You never have to show the list to anyone. Now write the names of ten people who are close to you in the second column. Finally, read your belief statement and the name of the person next to it and place a check in the third column if this also describes what you know about your significant person's belief. You will need to repeat this for each of your beliefs if you really want to have an in-depth picture of those around you.

I believe that...	Significant people in my life	Like me

I believe that...	Significant people in my life	Like me

Exercise B: Now repeat the same procedure for your values. In this case, you will identify your own values system by completing the statement beginning with, "It's important for me to..." "It's important for me to feel safe" or "It's important for me to be noticed." Once you have done this, use a word or short phrase to capture what is beneath that statement. It may be "security" or "recognition from others." Create your framework using the same two columns as before. At the end of this exercise, you will have a much better idea as to who is in your circle of influence and why your life looks the way it does.

Values

It's important for me to...	Underlying need	Significant people in my life	Like me

Affirmation:

I surround myself with individuals who encourage me to dream big and to pursue my goals with unwavering conviction.

You are more likely to feel self-confident when those around you offer their support and understanding. Take time to listen to their conversations about how they describe their own path in life and how well that matches what they are doing to realize it. Do they share grandiose dreams followed by a litany of reasons as to why they will never come true? I meet with several colleagues one-on-one on a regular basis to set goals and develop plans for achieving them. Writing this book is one of them. We hold each other accountable for taking the steps we discuss and explore ways to overcome any obstacles that arise.

One of my beliefs was based on my experience with my college English teacher who displayed my first writing assignment to the class with a large red F on it, declaring to my classmates that this was a prime example of how NOT to write a paper. I told myself that writing was not a strength that kept me from venturing into this unknown territory for years. My colleagues suggested I look into hiring a writing coach who would provide the encouragement, structure, and guidance I needed. I followed their advice and worked every day to make this goal a reality.

You may also discover that there are people in your life who are draining you of your energy because their beliefs and values are not congruent with yours. They are always finding reasons why you should forego what you want in life. Their motives for doing so may be based on their wanting to protect you from disappointment and pain. They fail to realize that you can recover from disappointments in life much easier than living in the regret that you never tried to begin with. Imagine your future as a series of "If onlys." "If only I had accepted that position when they offered it to me." "If only I had finished my degree." "If only I had moved across the country when I was younger."

Then there are those with an agenda based on envy for the life they never had. Why should you be successful when they passed up those opportunities and were now miserable with their current state? When you identify such people from your lists, ask yourself what they are adding to the life you see yourself living. Based on your answer you may wish to distance yourself from their influence. You will have feelings related to loss if this happens, but eventually, you will see the effects of releasing them to their own choices. You will also have room to attract people who are more positive in their perspective.

Key Learning Points

- Self-confidence develops over time with experience and success.
- When Plan A does not work out, move on to Plan B.
- Life is not compartmentalized. One aspect of life affects each of the others.
- Learning occurs on both a formal and an informal level.
- What a person thinks about themselves is a filter for how they experience life.
- Gratitude opens the door to possibility.
- Successful people spend time in the company of other successful people.

What is your story around self-confidence as you read through this chapter? What was it that triggered your thoughts around this? Write your thoughts below.

CHAPTER THREE

Perseverance

"With ordinary talent and extraordinary perseverance, all things are attainable."
– Thomas Foxwell Buxton

Perseverance self-assessment quiz

Mark **Yes** or **No** as it applies to your life today.

1. I am able to stay focused even when there are distractions.	Yes	No
2. I generally have a plan for completing a project.	Yes	No
3. When I face an obstacle I consider my options for moving forward.	Yes	No
4. I can alter my goals based on my assessment of new information.	Yes	No
5. I feel a sense of accomplishment and pride when I complete a task.	Yes	No
6. I view taking on a new task as an opportunity to learn.	Yes	No
7. I can determine when it's most effective for me to work alone or with others.	Yes	No
8. I can break up tasks into doable steps.	Yes	No
9. I can survive setbacks.	Yes	No
10. I seek out individuals who I perceive as successful in what they do.	Yes	No

To determine your score, count the number of **Yes** statements. ____

8-10 You indicate a **high** degree of ability within this area.

4-7 You indicate a **moderate** degree of ability within this area.

1-3 You indicate a **low** degree of ability within this area.

Perseverance defined

When you possess clarity and firmness of purpose, you know what you're aiming for and you figure out how to obtain it. It requires persistence and tenacity no matter what challenges and obstacles you may encounter. Perseverance describes a continued effort to move towards a goal even when it is difficult or takes longer than anticipated.

When I chose to pursue a doctorate, I had no idea what that journey would be like. Most people earn this degree in a few years. That was not the case for me. My first step was to complete all of the required courses. It meant studying for exams, writing papers, and delivering projects while working in a full-time job. Looking back, I don't remember any of those tasks being particularly easy, especially the statistics classes.

What was supposed to take a few years stretched into ten, and there was still the dissertation to write. A move from Arizona to California after my coursework was done coincided with preparation for my written and oral qualifying exams. In addition to the adjustment to a new position and surroundings, there were what seemed like endless hours of studying and poring through more research to pass those two requirements. During this time my interest in the entire project would wax and wane.

Hiring a dissertation coach and setting up a system in which I had to pay a specific amount for every day I didn't write provided little motivation. It was amazing how creative I could be in finding ways to avoid working on the dissertation. After almost eight years, the University informed me that, if I didn't finish this in one year, I would be dropped from the program. Needless to say, that was the impetus needed to apply my full attention to its completion.

Could I have finished the program sooner? Most likely I could have, but at the same time, there were new situations that presented themselves that expedited the process. Advancements in technology allowed me to reach a wider potential set of participants for the study, giving me a sample that exceeded most other studies in my field. New software was now available that would take all of my information and format it to align with University standards for publishing dissertations. Through serendipity, I met someone who lived less than a mile from me whose expertise was in statistical analysis. She steered me in the right direction in how to analyze and present all the data I had collected. All that was required of me was to stay focused on my goal and take one step at a time toward achieving it. Of course, there were times when it would have been easier to abandon this goal, but the end result was worth it.

This is my story about my experience with perseverance and its benefit in my life. It's not an isolated incident but merely one that left the greatest impression. Other pursuits have fallen along the wayside, like learning to become an accomplished pianist or designing skyscrapers. Neither of those pursuits was rooted in the experience needed for success. To be an accomplished pianist required dedicated practice time that I was unwilling to give. Designing skyscrapers meant completing a degree in architecture which involved advanced mathematical training. That was not my forte. It's important to delineate between goals supported by actions and possibilities that are nothing more than flights of fancy.

Life would flow easier if you were cognizant of the exact moment of the next beginning. Transitions don't always have a specific time attached to them unless you know for certain that the next step already is in place. You may have ended one job on a Friday with a new one starting in two weeks. Many times you don't have that luxury. You're informed on Friday that you will be out of work starting on Monday, and there is nothing on the horizon to replace it. After the initial shock subsides, you begin to gather your wits and begin to plan your uncertain future. What do you do first? Make the call to initiate your unemployment benefits or head to the local bar to drown your sorrows? How long will it be before you can find a job that can provide some stability in your life? This is the time that perseverance comes into play. You will need to tap into it to survive your untimed sojourn. Here are some suggestions for how to do that.

> *"It's time to buckle down and do this thing! I have the skills and tools to do this, to succeed, so just get on with it."*
> – JC, Director, Product Management

Live one day at a time

> *"I barely have time to think. But the best way to stay grounded is to take it one day at a time."*
> – Alessia Cara

There are entire programs that exist in the world today based on the premise that the way to accomplish anything in life is to focus only on the day you have before you. In Alcoholics Anonymous the key to staying sober is to refrain from drinking that day only. Eventually, those days stretch into weeks, months, and years. There will be days that feel like they will never end and days that flow easily. The emphasis is not on what your life will be like twenty-four years from now, but what it takes to make it through the next 24 hours. The future will take care of itself. Remind yourself that you can do just about anything if it has a set beginning and end.

As a human being, you have been given the gift of foresight. You have also been given the gift of choice that allows you to create in your mind what that future will look like. That future can be as short as ten minutes from now. You can shift forward into hyperdrive with your story to devise an outcome of how your life will be based on how life looks at the moment. One question that people pose when faced with an ominous outcome is, "What's the worst that can happen?" My response was always the same, "I'll die from making that choice." Obviously, that was a convenient way to avoid making a choice. The reality was that if you didn't make the choice, it would most likely be made for you. If you're having a particularly hard day you can always stop and reset the clock in your head and start fresh. It can make a difference in what you do next. It gives you the feeling that you are back in control of your life. Even the most thoroughly developed goals are subject to being carried out one day at a time.

> *"Take it one step at a time. There are things*
> *beyond our control even if we have done all we can.*
> *We just accept what happened and move on*
> *to new ventures. It's a journey that we experience.*
> *– AW*

Exercise: Choose five tasks related to one of your goals that you will focus on in the next 24 hours. Place a checkmark in the Completed column when you have accomplished the task. Notice how you feel as you check off each task.

Goal:	
Task	**Completed**
1.	
2.	
3.	
4.	
5.	

Some people place post-its where they can serve as visible reminders of staying in the moment. The fewer words, the better. "Focus." "Keep it simple." "Small steps." "Remember to breathe." Any time you find yourself projecting into the future with self-defeating thoughts, redirect your attention with these post-its. If you're concerned about what others might think if they saw them on the wall or on your computer at your workstation, don't be; it might be just what your co-workers need to help them survive the stresses that are keeping them from performing at optimal level.

What happens when the day seems more like it's controlling you than you are controlling it? Should you think that you have taken on more than you can handle, consider breaking it into doable pieces and then throw yourself into it. Rather than feel defeated or overwhelmed by it, you can take ownership of those pieces. For example, you may have a project that requires you to produce a major document. You don't have a clue where to begin. Refer to your goals in the above exercise. Choose one of them and list the steps you would need to take to move forward to achieve your goal.

Perhaps your goal is to write a book about successful people. Your task might be to decide on a format for the book. Think about what might be paralyzing to the process and plan around it. When you find yourself in this state, you could begin with collecting and reviewing similar books to see how they are formatted. Then you could decide which format best matches what you hope to communicate to the reader. You can break each step needed to obtain your goal of publishing a book into smaller ones to make them doable and manageable. Don't worry about whether it's right or wrong; just take action toward your goal.

Exercise: Ask yourself what you envision as a career-related goal in any area of your life. Write your goal as specifically as possible. It may be "I am working as a financial consultant with 10 paying clients by October 1, 20 . Now write down at least three action steps you can take today to achieve that goal. You may want to write them on an index card and keep them in your wallet or purse for review three times a day. Commit to taking the actions needed that day to achieve your goal.

Affirmation:

I embrace the power of living one day at a time during my job search, knowing that each day is an opportunity for progress and growth.

Challenge counterproductive beliefs

"Negative thoughts stick around because we believe them,
not because we want them or choose them."
– Andrew J. Bernstein

You live in a world that is constantly bombarding you with information. That information comes in the form of physical sensations and both verbal and nonverbal messages. What physical sensations tell you is whether something is cold or hot, its distance from you, or if it's a source of pain or comfort. We then respond accordingly, based on prior knowledge of and biological reactions to its effects. We develop belief systems needed for survival and self-preservation. Examples of these are "Applying too much pressure with your finger against a sharp object will produce pain," "Staring directly into the sun will damage your vision," and "Trying to cross a railroad track when the train is less than fifty feet from you will likely result in your death." These are what we refer to as productive beliefs. There aren't too many exceptions to what occurs when you act counter to these beliefs.

Counterproductive beliefs are generated within a society or culture over time. They may be based on the experiences of a group reacting to circumstances within a specific time in history or an attempt to control certain classes of people. They appear to originate from a societal concern that limits rather than expands potential contributions and prevents you from exercising options that would be within your best interest. They warp your view of the world and how you're expected to function within it. Those beliefs that challenge your logical approach to life would include "No one hires anyone who is older than 50" and "Girls shouldn't consider careers in math and sciences."

Exercise: List specific beliefs that you hold that are affecting your achievement of goals in various parts of your life. Next, describe how they have been limiting your progress toward those goals. Finally, write a new belief that would support you having what you want. Here is an example of what that might look like:

Counterproductive belief	How it limits what I want in life	My new supportive belief
Employers don't consider people over 50 for job openings in today's market.	I remain unemployed for months. I feel depressed and don't actively seek employment. I spend my time blaming potential employers for age discrimination, making me a victim.	I have a wealth of experience and marketable skills that qualify me for current job openings.
Counterproductive belief	**How it limits what I want in life**	**My new supportive belief**
Counterproductive belief	**How it limits what I want in life**	**My new supportive belief**

Counterproductive belief	**How it limits what I want in life**	**My new supportive belief**
Counterproductive belief	**How it limits what I want in life**	**My new supportive belief**

Now let's look at what verbal and nonverbal messages convey and contribute to your belief system. You begin life by processing nonverbal information. One of the first nonverbals that you take in is what you observe in the face of your primary caretaker. In most cases, this is your mother. It's not by accident that our eyes are the most contrasting feature on our faces. The eyes capture the attention of a newborn and communicate a variety of messages, ranging from warmth to disapproval. The same is true of the human voice.

A simple statement such as, "I love you," can be inflected to show deep affection, commitment, playfulness, or even pleading. What is needed is the ability to correctly interpret what underlies the nonverbals being sent to you. This is when you begin to create your cognitive belief systems. When a parent's "I love you" is paired with a negative behavior such as a look of disdain or lack of physical contact, the child begins to equate love with unworthiness. When this occurs with any regularity, the message becomes internalized as a counterproductive belief. "I am unworthy of being loved" or "Any type of physical contact is better than none" which can lead to entry into unhealthy relationships.

The same process of internalizing what you hear and perceive is true for statements related to judgments about your abilities. What begins as youthful optimism regarding our capacity to perform superhuman feats becomes shaped by the messages of those around us. "You're not very good at that" "You'll hurt yourself if you try that" and "Maybe you could try something easier" influence the choices you make. These statements contribute to your belief system, and youthful optimism fades into limiting future activities. While there are statements made to you directly on a personal level, you're also hearing messages about a specific subgroup to which you have been assigned based on factors such as gender, age, ethnicity, and so on. These messages were what guided women into occupations such as teacher and nurse based on "Girls are better suited for professions in which they are caring for others."

The airwaves are filled with an often-heard statement from those over a certain age that "No one will hire me because I am over fifty, and employers probably think I came from the Dark Ages of technology." There is also a tendency to categorize the types of careers people should pursue based on their ethnic backgrounds. You can take these messages and use them to justify your lack of progress or you can create new ones that support who you are and what you have to offer. This is the time that perseverance comes into play in holding your course in spite of what you have heard in the past. Take time to write out the list of beliefs that you have internalized and consciously work to eliminate those that are unproductive. This is what we learned in psychology class to be known as "thought stopping." As soon as the unproductive thought enters your mind, stop it and replace it with a healthier one. After a while, the new thought will be programmed as a natural response to what is occurring.

> *"[I] work to assess my skills and how I effectively applied them in a job environment. [I] always learn from mistakes I may have made—how in the next job I could approach the same challenges differently and learn not to make the same mistake or preferably approach the situation as a new challenge."*
> — LS, Project Manager and Business Analyst

Affirmation:

I release beliefs that no longer serve me, knowing that the world is filled with abundance and possibilities waiting to be explored.

Cultivate tenacity

*"Let me tell you the secret that has led me to my goal.
My strength lies solely in my tenacity."*
– Louis Pasteur

There will be days when the only word that seems to exist is "NO." "No, we are not looking for someone with your background." "No, that idea will never catch on." "No, we haven't had time to read your resume." One story that emerges related to facing the "NOs" in our lives is that of Walt Disney when he was attempting to fund his first theme park. The story goes that he was rejected by 302 lending institutions after pitching his concept for Disneyland before one lender finally said, "Yes." It might not have helped that he had filed for bankruptcy several times as a young man. To an outsider, Walt might have looked like a loser, but in his mind, he only saw a winner. Imagine how passionate Walt must have been to be told time after time that his plan had little chance of succeeding. What would have happened if he had put his dreams away in the 1950s after the first "No" was delivered? In spite of the number of rejections he received, he pushed forward against the odds. Today there are five Disney-related theme parks located around the world employing close to 200,000 workers. Perhaps Walt's journey was the inspiration for the song that tells us that when you wish upon a

> *"I am realizing that I can and will be successful. My tenacity and hope will be essential ingredients to endure and obtain the job that I dream [of] and the life that I want."*
> – MM, Program Manager

star, your dreams come true. This is but one tale of how a vision can become reality when tenacity is applied.

I'm sure that Walt Disney didn't walk into those lending institutions without a plan in hand. Remember that a dream without a plan is just a dream. Plans are subject to revision based on new information. The greatest discoveries and inventions were the result of modifications by the visionary that would improve the efficiency or utility of their work. Even with the most solid plan in hand, unforeseen circumstances intervene leaving the creator to wonder if this was a good idea to begin with. We know that opening day at Disneyland did not go the way Walt had envisioned it. There were problems with drinking fountains, rides breaking down, and the extreme heat turning the asphalt into a nightmare for women in heels. That didn't deter Walt from returning to the drawing board to correct those problems.

So what do you do with the "NOs" in your life, especially when you hear a string of them? Do you decide to give up your goal, or do you continue asking, as Walt Disney did? What would have happened if Walt had given up after the 301st request? There would be no Magic Kingdom or Epcot Center to visit. The thousands of jobs that were created to build Disneyland and Disney World would never have been needed. The joy on the faces of children (and adults) that are continually in awe of the wonders they experience on their vacations would be missing. That vision kept Walt's dream alive.

Another example of how tenacity works comes from Jack Canfield, noted author and international speaker. In 1991 Jack and his partner, Mark Victor Hansen, were searching for a publisher for their newly written book, *Chicken Soup for the Soul*. It took 144 rejections over an eight-month period before a struggling publications firm agreed to take it on. Today *Chicken Soup for the Soul* has exceeded 500 million copies sold. What would the fate of that book have been had they stopped searching after the first "NO?"

When you're going through changes and challenges in your life, hold fast to what matters most to you, much like Walt Disney or Jack Canfield did. Each of us holds a vision of what our own Disneyland or bestseller would be. It could be living out your dream of a job that allows you to make a significant difference for children, inventing a device that can defy gravity, or performing life-saving surgeries. When you hear a "No," conjure up an image of Walt Disney or Jack Canfield and move on to your next possibility; ask until you hear a "YES." If you firmly believe in your vision, you will eventually meet at least one other person who shares it with you.

The result may be a new position, a chance to start your own business, or an offer to participate in an entirely new venture.

Exercise: Think of something that you wanted in your lifetime.

On a scale of 1 (Low) to 10 (High), how badly did you want it?

____

What actions did you take to get it?

____

____

____

How long did it take for you to have it in your life? ____________

____

____

What obstacles did you face in working to get it? _______________

____

____

What motivated you to keep working toward getting it?___________

____

____

How did you feel when you finally had it in your life?____________

____

____

Affirmation:

I trust that my tenacity will lead me to the right opportunity as I build the foundation for a successful and fulfilling career.

Work with a mentor

*"There is nothing I like better than conversing
with aged men. For I regard them as travelers who have
gone a journey which I too may have to go, and of whom
I ought to inquire whether the way is smooth and
easy or rugged and difficult. Is life harder toward the end,
or what report do you give it?"*
– Plato

There is something to be said for the lessons that come with experience. Without the guidance of someone who knows the slippery slopes and political machinations of the workplace, you may find yourself repeating behaviors that could eventually have you packing your belongings and being escorted out the back door. In the past your supervisor most likely served as that guide, assisting you in problem solving and acting as a sounding board for bouncing off ideas and determining whether or not to promote them. In today's world, a long-standing relationship with a supervisor is more the exception than the rule. Either you or your supervisor carries an expiration date for that position, whether it be voluntary or involuntary. Today's mentors can come from the ranks of those currently or previously employed by an organization or from outside the company in the same field as you are.

The positive outcomes of working with a mentor are an increase in income, handling the politics of the organization, a better understanding of the company's culture, and higher productivity. Working with a mentor reduces your stress levels because you don't need to second-guess your actions. While the value of having a mentor is unquestionable, finding one who is right for you requires planning and effort. You will need to consider the background and experience you require of a potential mentor. The candidate may be likable yet lacking the knowledge necessary to walk you through a situation with a suitable outcome. You also want to identify how the mentor shares information. Is the communication style too directing, ambivalent, or laissez-faire? Ask yourself which style will contribute most to your own professional growth. If you're working with a mentor who spoon-feeds your every action for a project or a problem, how will this benefit you when the mentor is not accessible?

In determining who to approach to serve as a mentor, ask yourself the following questions about the potential mentor's qualities:

1. How well does the person communicate? Does he or she have the time to devote to this type of relationship?

2. How structured will the mentoring sessions be? Will the mentor know in advance what issues will be discussed during the mentoring session? How much advance notice will be provided to give the mentor time to think about strategies and resources?

3. How does the mentor demonstrate success in his or her chosen field?

4. How direct and straightforward will the mentor be in addressing concerns and strategies? How will suggestions be delivered so that the person being mentored feels in control of the situation and does not feel obligated to follow directives given by the mentor?

5. How will the mentor stay current with changes in the workplace? How will the mentor stay knowledgeable of trends, opportunities, and developments that affect your position?

6. How will the mentor retain objectivity and fairness when working together, understanding that there are no hidden agendas in the relationship?

Utilizing the talents of a mentor is most effective when you take on an active role in the relationship. You will need to have clearly established career goals and benchmarks for knowing where you are in your progress in achieving those goals. You may want to be focusing on your presentation or your negotiation skills. Spend some time observing and gathering information on senior staff who demonstrate competence in the areas you identify. Approach the potential mentor by pointing out what you have specifically observed and the impression it has made on you before posing your request to have them consider being your mentor. The person may ask for some time to consider your invitation, especially if there is the matter of the time involved. Allow for that and set a date for the decision to be made. Don't give up if the response you hear is, "Thanks for thinking of me, but I just don't have the time to devote to this." If the person cannot make that commitment, ask if he or she knows of someone else who might fill that role. This is where perseverance comes into play.

Historically, males have accessed mentor relationships making it easier to pursue this opportunity. If you identify with a group other than this, think about the issues facing you. Are you seeing opportunities for promotions passing you by or cultural nuances that affect communication? Perhaps finding a mentor with whom you share these issues based on a commonality such as gender or ethnicity would be helpful. Again, you will need to do your homework in seeking out those individuals who are most representative of your needs and goals. It may be necessary at this point to find someone who meets these criteria from outside your current work setting. What is important are the qualities and competencies you're seeking and the mentor's ability to share those in a way that you can incorporate them into your identity.

> *"I find that confiding in someone with the troubles I had is very useful. I find being honest about distracting helps me keep them [my troubles] at bay."*
> – RW, Data engineer

Using the services of a mentor can be helpful when you're considering a change from one field to another. You may possess a clear understanding of how to function in your current position, but the playing field shifts significantly when you're the new kid on the block. This may be even more so if you're making such a change later in your career. If you're making the transition after holding higher-level positions, you may not be making a move to one equal to or higher than that one. When I made a decision to leave the field of education and pursue career coaching, I moved from administration to direct service to clients. It also meant a significant reduction in pay. Having colleagues who had worked in the field for years available to discuss the best way to advance made the transition easier and tempered my expectations with a more realistic view of how this could work.

You might ask yourself, "Why would someone take the time to mentor me?" Mentors derive satisfaction from watching you grow. They also expand their knowledge of the company and its internal workings when they are sharing in a problem-solving session. Remember that learning is a two-way street, so mentors can also learn what the latest trends are in technology and work habits of those in younger generations. It can also rekindle the spark of what motivated them to join the company or enter the field in the first place.

Exercise: List three attributes you're looking for in a mentor.

1. ____

2. ____

3. ____

Name three people you know who possess those attributes. Circle Yes or No if you know them personally.

1. ____ Yes   No

2. ____ Yes   No

3. ____ Yes   No

If you know them personally, what is your plan for approaching them to be your mentor? Next to each person write the date by which you will contact him or her.

Date

Person A: _______________________________________

____

____

Person B: _______________________________________

____

____

Person C: _______________________________________

____

____

If you don't know the person personally, who do you know who could introduce you to them? Next to each person write the date by which you will contact him or her.

Date:

Person A: ____

Person B: ____

Person C: ____

Once you have identified your mentor, what is your plan to work together to accomplish your goals?

____

____

____

____

____

Affirmation:

I embrace the opportunity to work with a mentor, benefitting from their insights, advice, and constructive feedback.

Market yourself

"Smile when they want you to frown, be happy
when they expect you to be sad, laugh when they think
you'll cry. Don't live based on what others think or
try to fit in, but always be in the best of yourself;
that's what makes you outstanding.
– Blaze Olamiday

Who you are differentiates you from everyone else who has lived or will live on this planet. You have been bestowed with a unique set of gifts and talents that you'll carry with you through life. It's your responsibility to know what those gifts and talents are and to be willing to share that with the world in a humble manner. Think about people you know who begin each sentence with "I." "I don't think there is anyone else who can perform at the level I do." "I am fully responsible for the success of this project." "I don't take 'no' for an answer." Their marketing plan is to elevate themselves at the expense of others. Sharing is not about being boastful. It's about recognizing that, when you place your gifts and talents in the service of others, there is no need to publicize them to the world. They will speak for themselves.

Many people are clueless as to what their major strengths are. One way to begin to identify them is to write down what you find yourself to be good at that requires little, if any, effort. These are called your natural talents. Your natural talents might include expressing yourself through writing, debugging a computer program, or finding a destination with little external information.

How you present your gifts to the world is what is referred to as branding. When working with clients I have them solicit feedback from ten people they know both personally and professionally. They are to ask those people to identify three traits or characteristics that come to mind as soon as they hear their name. The next step is to look for patterns among the responses. Do words like caring, good listener, and generous show up on the list? Or perhaps analytical, inventive, and technically savvy are most prominent. How well do these words match your own description of how you think you come across to people? Is there a congruency with the two descriptions? If there isn't, what might be contributing to the disconnect between each of those viewpoints? This is the time to engage in introspection and decide what steps to take. If you consider yourself to be a caring and giving person, seek windows of opportunity for sharing through your actions. If you describe yourself as innovative, look for ways to demonstrate that trait. It can be in the workplace or while volunteering. People will notice if you're consistent in showing up as the person you are. You should be a walking advertisement for your brand.

Your brand is what you take into your job interview, how you can be expected to act at work, and what future tasks can be assigned to you. You're constantly sending out branding messages whether you're aware of them or not. If you want to see how potent they are, identify one person you know with whom you work. Write three words or phrases that you would use to describe them. Your task is to observe them during the day and make a tally mark next to each trait as you observe the person demonstrating them. It's important to be as specific as possible with the traits you include so be sure to avoid words like "nice." At the end of the day, look at your list. How did the person fare in the marks you gave them?

What are the traits that have served you in surviving through difficult times? Optimism, resourcefulness, flexibility? Are these traits ones that others would readily use in describing you? Ask yourself how you have capitalized upon these traits to make it over the rough spots.

During a particularly difficult time in my late twenties, I felt a sense of anxiety permeating my life and I couldn't shake it. It was all I could do to just get through the day. It took every bit of energy within me to focus on doing my job. One November I sat in the back of our morning assembly that began the school day and realized I had nothing left to rely on. My present had no meaning or purpose, and I could see no future. A fellow teacher notified my supervisor of my situation, and she told me to go home and return to work when I was ready. I don't remember how I drove home or what I was to do next, but I knew something had to change. This loss of identity and purpose often constitutes the mindset of those going through a transition related to a job loss. It requires that a new identity and purpose emerge to replace the old one. I knew that I needed to take a serious look at the choices I had made up to this point and tap into an inner strength to proceed with my life. That attitude spurred me to make some significant adjustments in my life based on the trait of determination. Determination and resolve have served me well over the years.

Exercise: Write three words that you would use to describe yourself. Now ask ten people you know to do the same for you. They should represent various areas of your life including friends and family, coworkers, people who belong to the same professional organizations, players on a sports team, etc. Next, indicate how long they have known you.

Three descriptive words:							
Name	**How affiliated**	**Descriptors**	**Years known**				
			<1	**1-5**	**6-10**	**11-15**	**>15**

Three descriptive words:							
Name	**How affiliated**	**Descriptors**	**Years known**				
			<1	1-5	6-10	11-15	>15

Ask yourself how you would want to be seen in a specific environment such as work. How well does the feedback you received match what the environment would call for? What might you need to work on to project a different brand, or what might you choose to pursue based on your feedback from others?

Affirmation:

I use my unique skills, experiences, and qualities as powerful tools that make me a valuable candidate for a potential position.

Follow up

"Success comes from taking the initiative and following up... persisting... eloquently expressing the depth of your love. What simple action could you take today to produce new momentum toward success in your life?"
– Anthony Robbins

Have you ever made a connection with someone at a networking event, at work, or perhaps at a social event and found the interchange stimulating enough to end in a promise to extend it through a meeting over coffee, an email, or a telephone call? You initiate that follow up within 24 hours while it's fresh in your mind, hopeful that there will be a response. Then you wait and wait and wait. What happened to the initial enthusiasm you had when you agreed to stay in touch? You typically create a story as to what occurred for this result. It might go something like this: "The person was only being polite at the time and never really intended to continue the relationship." "After thinking about our conversation, he decided there wasn't anything of value that would promote his own agenda." Or "She's probably too busy to get back to me." In each case, you have stopped any forward momentum that was generated during that initial interaction. The story you created may or may not have validity attached to it. If it turns out that the other party truly was disinterested in pursuing anything further, you have to release that and move on. But what if the story proved otherwise? You will never know if you shut the door on opportunity prematurely.

Think about applying for a position just for practice. In one case the employer decided to extend the application deadline for another two months to increase the pool of applicants. Sometimes the employer will send an email or letter notifying you that you're not a match for what they are seeking. Most often you do not hear back from them. This is when a follow up from you would be helpful. A short message expressing your continued interest will keep you on their radar. Otherwise, the employer may think that you have secured employment elsewhere or are no longer interested in the position they are offering. When you're gathering information related to a potential change in occupation or are in the interview stage, there is always the question of the frequency of follow up messages with your contact. How many is too many? One approach is to continue to seek a response until one is received.

Follow up is all about your willingness to persevere in spite of what appears to be conflicting evidence. If you truly believe that there is something to be gained by both parties, consider pursuing an answer for as long as fits your timeline of needs before putting it to rest. It's not unusual for the other person to express their appreciation for your continued efforts. People may not initially respond due to sickness, their need to focus on a project that is deadline-driven, emails going into spam, or a family emergency. It's important that your subsequent communication not contain references to your irritation or disappointment in the other person's timeliness. That tone will not be taken favorably and it can contribute to the demise of that relationship. Stay positive and upbeat each time you reach out to them.

You can develop the habit of follow up if it's not in your nature to do so. This was one behavior that needed a major overhaul in my own life. For me to make that change required the willingness to root out its cause. For me, the root cause related to lack of clarity in what steps I was to take. That might have been the result of insufficient information or the lack of a plan. To remedy this bad habit I had to swallow my humble pill and acknowledge that help was needed in this area. With a few successes I discovered that there was no magic behind this. One strategy that worked for me was to make a verbal promise to the other person to contact them within a specific time period and repeating that promise prior to our ending that interaction. Then I would either write their name in my appointment book or place their business card in front of my computer once I arrived home. I consciously plan what I need to say, beginning with an appreciation for the time spent together. Then I propose the next steps that we will take in building our relationship. This has often led to long-lasting bonds, while other times it has been shorter in duration but still worth the effort expended.

Some people ask if there is a window beyond which follow up is no longer possible. My response is that there is always the chance that a relationship can be rekindled. The way to do that is to first recognize and take responsibility for the lapse in communication. This is not intended as an excuse but more as a willingness to reconnect. Inform the other person of what has been happening in your life and make sure that you ask the same of them. Set up a time to talk either face to face or on the telephone to catch up. If for any reason the other person is not open to continuing the relationship, acknowledge that and wish them well. Then ask yourself what you have learned from this that you can handle differently in the future.

Exercise: Following is a sample form for tracking your plan to follow up with contacts. Feel free to use it as is or adapt it to your needs. If you have the capability of creating this system on your computer or phone, then use whatever system works best for you.

Name and organization	Phone Number/ Email	Purpose	Today's Date	Follow-up Date	Comments

Affirmation:

I recognize the importance of follow up in my job search recognizing that it is a powerful tool that demonstrates my professionalism, enthusiasm, and genuine interest in the opportunities I pursue.

Establish a support system

*"A career in sport is almost impossible to
manage without the support, and guidance,
and reassurance of family and friends. During tough times,
and there always are, this is whom we go to."*
– Rahul Dravid

There is something to be said about the value of having one or more people in your life who you can rely on to bolster you when you're feeling down. These people are there for you in a variety of ways and sometimes show up when you least expect it and need it most. They can be family members, close friends, classmates, colleagues, coaches, and even total strangers. My experiences sitting next to strangers on an airplane confirms that this can happen. On my return home following my mother's funeral, I just happened to be seated next to someone who had gone through a similar experience, and his words provided the hope and comfort I needed to make it through those otherwise hours of loneliness and loss as I returned home. At the same time, I have been the one to offer support. It may have been related to work issues or a relationship. Most of the time support meant serving as a nonjudgmental listener. These situations are reminders that you're always given what you need at the moment to face the challenge before you.

> *"I've had to repeat my story over and over again.*
> *A few of my "relatives" (not related) ask about me and*
> *are concerned. My parents seem concerned, but don't*
> *ask how I am doing. The hardest part is how it*
> *impaired my parents and other colleagues who I*
> *thought would have reached out to me."*
> – AH, Principal, Customer Engagement Specialist

You might ask yourself why it would be important to have a support group when you're ultimately responsible for what happens in your life. It's true that you're the one in charge of where your destiny takes you. There will be times when you're uncertain as to the direction it can take. When you find yourself in this predicament, your support system is there to guide and encourage you. Without them, you have a tendency to adopt counterproductive mechanisms such as procrastination and self-defeating talk. You can't see any further than the obstacle before you so you either ignore its presence or engage in activities to distract you. These activities include excessively watching television, playing online games for hours, sleeping for ten or more hours at a time, or consuming foods high in fat and sugar, justifying them as comfort food. When you find yourself heading in this direction, your support system is there to refocus you and get you back on track.

Who are the people in your life that you can turn to for support? Think of key people and the role they played in helping you over the rough spots. Realize that some people are better at work issues while others do better when relationships are problematic. You may discover that you need to develop several support systems specific to what is facing you in life. It might be helpful to list the major areas of your life like Career, Relationships, Finances, Leisure, Social Causes, Spiritual Growth, and then identify the people who support you in successfully achieving the goals you have set around them. This will also assist in evaluating whether you need to expand or reduce the number included based on how well they are doing. The members of your support system will likely change over time as you evolve as a person. It's more the exception than the rule to maintain an intact system throughout your life.

Exercise: On the following page, make a list of people in your life who are there for you when you need support. Place an X in each box that corresponds to the type(s) of support they provide. As situations occur during your transition, consciously reach out to the appropriate people listed.

Name	Emotional Support	Informational Support	Constructive Feedback	Fun and Recreation

One form of support that is especially helpful when you're dealing with career issues is a success team. Ideally, this is generally a group consisting of up to eight people who assemble on a regular basis to check in on the commitments they have made during their prior meeting. It serves as a way to hold people accountable and to provide suggestions and resources when obstacles occur. It also functions to celebrate the victories that members make along the way whether they are large or small. Sometimes the group will identify a topic that is pertinent to what each of them is facing in the workplace. It might be how to deal with unsupportive managers, strategies for meeting deadlines, or how and when to say "no" to tasks that take you away from your primary responsibilities. The discussions around these topics are designed to maximize job performance and minimize venting and complaining.

> *"I've immersed myself doing volunteer work that I really enjoy. I'm making sure not to lose contact with friends in my social circle, even though I'm not gainfully employed."*
> – EY, Graphic Artist

Members of the success team are free to contact one another between sessions if needed, and they know that they will be sharing their progress at the next regularly scheduled meeting. These support groups can serve to assist participants when they are seeking employment as well as develop and hone skills for those currently working. The group members can represent a variety of occupations or can be limited to those in the same profession.

As you become more comfortable within a support system, consider finding an accountability partner. This is a person with whom you develop a relationship built on deep trust and respect. I attended a networking event and met a gentleman who I thought might be a good person with whom to have a conversation. It turned out that we had more in common than I would have thought. We were the same age, grew up in the same state, and shared a passion for coaching. We agreed to have coffee leading to a weekly get together in which we set goals and discussed various ways to achieve them. This relationship continued for several years. If we were working on a project such as a presentation, we reviewed the content and suggested ways to improve the delivery. We counted upon each other to challenge a commitment we had made and were not following through on. Oftentimes we learned that the resistance was due to lack of a skill or information. Talking through it leads to identifying resources and strategies for moving forward.

There will be days when you think you can tackle anything that comes your way, and there will be days when you have serious doubts about yourself. When feelings of depression or uncertainty emerge, reach out to someone in your network and talk it through. Discuss your worst fears and find a way to confront them. It's often a matter of moving from a looming problem to a workable solution. When the issues extend beyond what someone in your support system can address, think about using professional support through counseling or coaching.

Affirmation:

With a network of support, I am better equipped to navigate challenges and seize opportunities, allowing me to achieve success in my job search.

Tap into a greater source

"Whatever the present moment contains, accept it as if you had chosen it. Always work with it, not against it."
— Eckhart Tolle

When feelings of isolation and hopelessness begin to set in, it helps to remember that you can tap into something greater than yourself. If you're a person who is so inclined to seek guidance from a power outside yourself, you may decide to access prayer as a way to survive life's challenges. For me, growing up in a specific religion meant instruction in a formal set of prayers. Once I learned them verbatim, I could recite them without ever giving attention to the meaning behind them. It wasn't until my adult years that I began to see prayer as a way to communicate with something greater than myself. That "something" continues to evolve for me. The approach to this concept is a choice for each individual. You may be a person who chooses to place complete responsibility for what happens in your life on yourself alone. It is whatever works in your life.

> *"[The] process [of] looking gets very old, very fast. All of it is on me with little to no support."*
> – LS, Project Manager

When your options for paying the rent or putting food on the table seem to be nonexistent, you may ask for intervention to change the situation. I have heard stories about how a problem seeming to have no solution was given an answer. I recall a time when I arrived home one afternoon from the movies to see what looked like Niagara Falls pouring over my carport. An upstairs toilet tank had burst while I was out and water was gushing in every possible direction. After turning off the water, I assessed the structural damage, which was considerable. Carpets were sopping wet, the drywall was ruined, and the subflooring was soaked. I contacted my insurance company and the bank to determine the cost for repairs. In the end, I decided to remodel my home based on advice I had received.

The result was that I was faced with expenses far beyond what my income could support. After speaking to a debt consolidation agent and an attorney who specialized in these types of situations, I was told there was no way out of this. I was desperate and could see no logical way to resolve my situation. That was when I decided to ask for guidance from my higher power. After sitting quietly with the problem, the solution appeared. With a few simple steps, I was able to pay off the entire debt within three years at minimal cost. The people I had originally spoken to suggested I write a book on this since they had never heard of anyone accomplishing something like this. I didn't write the book, but I certainly learned a lot in the process.

> *"[I] leaned on God's wisdom and promises that He knows what's best for my life. He knows the past, present, and future and [I] trust in him. When he closes a door, He is protecting me from something and He will open a door that is better. [I] pray to God for His guiding, intervention, and divine appointment and divine favors."*
> — SP, Ballet Instructor

Maybe tapping into something greater than yourself is about releasing control and allowing yourself to become open to possibilities. I don't claim to be an expert on how it works, only that it may be worth a try when you feel like you're out of options.

You may feel or think that this moment will never end, but it will. Think about times in the past when you told yourself that your current situation was forever. Then look at your life today and identify its effect on how you view the world. Remember that what is happening now doesn't define your life. All you need do is to stay in the moment and take care of what is in front of you. The old adage of "This too shall pass" can carry you through the rough times in life.

Exercise: If you have a belief in something greater than yourself, take time to write a letter to the source asking for what you need. Begin with "Dear______." Use this exercise as an opportunity to specify what it is that you want and/or need at this time. The clearer you are in your asking, the more likely you will be to receive it. You may also add a date by which you would like it to be delivered. I always add, "This or something better" at the end of it. When you have written it, put a date on it and place it in a container where it will remain unread. You may be tempted to take it out and read it. Resist the temptation and allow the solution to show up. Don't worry about how that will happen. Trust that it will be acted upon.

Affirmation:

I trust that the job I seek aligns with my highest good and am open to synchronicities and signs that guide me towards the right opportunities and connections.

Key Learning Points

- Combining clarity and perseverance increases the likelihood of meeting one's goals.
- Feedback in any form can contribute to personal and professional growth.

- Success in life is not a solo sport, but the result of team effort.
- Branding communicates how each person shows up for life on a daily basis.
- Integrity is measured by consistency between one's words and actions.

OUT OF WORK... NOT OUT OF WORTH

What is your story around perseverance as you read through this chapter? What was it that triggered your thoughts around this?

CHAPTER FOUR

Acceptance

*"Sometimes you just have to regret things
and move on."*
– Charlaine Harris

Acceptance self-assessment quiz

Mark **Yes** or **No** as it applies to your life today.

1. I have a strong sense of who I am.	Yes	No
2. I don't take myself too seriously.	Yes	No
3. I accept that loss is part of life.	Yes	No
4. I have healthy coping mechanisms for dealing with my current emotional state.	Yes	No
5. I know what creates stress for me.	Yes	No
6. I know what my strengths are and use them in my daily life.	Yes	No
7. I am open to feedback on my limitations and blind spots.	Yes	No
8. I recognize that stress can have a negative effect on my health.	Yes	No
9. I know when I need to reach out to others for support.	Yes	No
10. I take responsibility for my actions.	Yes	No

To determine your score, count the number of **Yes** statements. ____

8-10 You indicate a **high** degree of ability within this area.

4-7 You indicate a **moderate** degree of ability within this area.

1-3 You indicate a **low** degree of ability within this area.

Acceptance defined

When you go through any form of change in your life, you will experience a range of thoughts and emotions surrounding it. Acceptance is the willingness to adjust to a situation. It begins with the initial shock that comes with whatever is confronting you. You may have learned that you are no longer employed, that your marriage of 26 years is over, or that your business partner has left the country with all of the company assets. These situations certainly constitute the more formidable events that you could face because of their rarity, and they would likely escalate your emotional level.

You probably do go through transition and change on a daily basis. You're running late for an important meeting because you can't find your car keys. You spill coffee on your shirt just before your interview. You forget to mail your insurance payment and are now outside your grace period. Regardless of their severity and impact on your life, these events all have one thing in common—a response to how you will deal with what comes next. At this point, there is nothing you can do to change what preceded the event. You can scream and swear, which may relieve the stress for the moment, but ultimately it's necessary to accept the reality of the situation and move on. How long that process will take is entirely in your hands.

I liken the process of acceptance to being dragged behind a moving vehicle. It will only persist for as long as you hold on to the rope. You're free to release it whenever you want. Unless you're a person who enjoys being in pain, letting go always feels better. I look back on situations in which I could have let go much sooner. I now realize that what kept me attached was adopting a victim mentality. These are the times when we perceive our fate as being someone or something acting to create misery in our lives. It becomes easier to blame external circumstances than to accept responsibility for initiating changes to minimize or avoid them in the future.

One reminder of how this works pertains to a business venture I pursued with someone I thought I could trust. After putting down a significant amount of money, I began to watch the assets being depleted by the other person's spending on personal items. It didn't take long to realize where this was headed. I ended the business relationship with a financial loss. When the experience repeated itself years later, I learned what the pattern was. I was sending out messages that I was fertile ground for these kinds of business arrangements. All the other person had to do was to gain my trust. It was a hard pill to swallow, but in accepting this about myself, I could consciously choose to decline the next offer. I will say that I was willing to pursue legal action which kept me from becoming a victim. It was up to me as to when I was ready and willing to let go of the rope. Along the way, I was aware of all the thoughts and emotions that surfaced and dealt with them to reduce their impact on me.

Face your losses

> *"Life seems sometimes like nothing more than*
> *a series of losses, from beginning to end. That's the given.*
> *How you respond to those losses, what you make of what's*
> *left, that's the part you have to make up as you go."*
> — Katharine Weber

For every end, there is a beginning. It's in the endings that we are forced to accept the reality that nothing is forever. For some people, endings signal a period of uncertainty and wondering when, and if, there will be something better awaiting them. For others, it can be a time of hope. Whatever has brought them to this moment is no longer present, and there is a belief that new situations will present themselves that bring joy and freedom. Between the ending and the beginning is that uncharted territory that must be navigated to reach the other side. You will likely experience the grieving process along the way. During this time it's perfectly natural to have strong emotions surfacing. If you have recently lost a job, or were passed over for a promotion, then that becomes your ending. This event will be followed by emotions such as shock, anger, betrayal, depression or perhaps even relief. You may replay the event repeatedly in your mind, somehow wanting to identify the one link in the chain of events that you could have changed that would have affected the outcome. You're powerless over the past. The ultimate reality is that you only have control over what is happening in the immediate moment.

We live in a society that characteristically defines who we are by what we do and whether or not we are doing it at the moment. One of the first questions that we are asked in a social or professional setting is, "What do you do?" The response that is expected is to state your current occupation. My experience in visiting other countries around the world is that this is not the first thing they want to know about you and that it would be considered bad manners to begin a conversation with this question. They tend to be more interested in your life in general. In this country when you're asked

> *"Realized that it wasn't ever going to get better, no matter how hard I tried or how much I worked. Should have left earlier and avoided the negative experiences."*
> – MW, Product Manager

about the status of your job or a promotion and you share the situation, you may feel ashamed, embarrassed, or apologetic if you don't fit an acceptable standard. When what you do for a living is reflected in your sense of self, the loss can be intensified. **Remind yourself that you are not your job**. Your job may serve as a source of validation for your skills and talents, but those skills and talents do not disappear when your job situation is affected.

Because so much time is spent in the workplace, it can serve as the hub of your social network. It's natural to form relationships with those who share common goals and experiences. It's also an opportunity to share what is referred to as "shop talk," the language of the workplace. If you aren't sure what "shop talk" is, just go to dinner or a party with a group of people you know who are outside your industry. They can easily slip into a verbiage that is totally foreign to you. That often happened when gathering with my fellow educators. We could go on for hours to the dismay of those around us who were clueless as to what and why we were discussing. When you are out or work, that camaraderie is no longer present. You can arrange to meet those with whom you worked to attempt to maintain that relationship, but soon the dynamics change to where you become the foreigner.

> *"I remind myself that it is not me. I have skills,*
> *lots of experience, and great success in my career.*
> *Someone else will see the great value I can provide."*
> — ML, IT Management

If you have worked for the same company for many years and this is the first time you have experienced unemployment, you may feel devastated. Many of my clients who had no idea that their positions were being terminated felt betrayed by their employers. They had given up to 25 years of their lives in support of their company and had nothing to show for it when work ended for them. Some of them believed that they would be employed in this position until they retired. Because of this belief they developed and used a limited number of skills to perform their job duties and had done nothing to update them.

Elisabeth Kübler-Ross, a Swiss-American psychiatrist who authored a ground-breaking book *On Death and Dying* in 1969, identified five stages that individuals go through in grieving a loss. Initially, the individual would experience a state of **denial** that the event was occurring.

> *"My initial emotional reaction was that of fear.*
> *Fear of the unknown, fear of loss and separation.*
> *Where do I go from here?"*
> – HJ, Teaching Professional

This was followed by **anger, bargaining, depression,** and eventually **acceptance**. There is no way to predict the speed at which each process will be completed. It's possible that the person may move through several stages and suddenly have an experience that causes a loop in the process.

The first reaction to loss is denial. This can't be happening to you. While many people view denial as a negative state, it's more likely the psyche creating a safety net that allows it to survive until it gathers enough information to take the next steps.

> *"I was in shock when I was told I was laid off after 17 years.*
> *I was in disbelief that I had been chosen.*
> *I was very sad that it was not my decision.*
> *I felt a complete lack of control and rejection."*
> *– JP*

Think about a time when you received a message that someone close to you had died. It can be such a shock to the system that you feel paralyzed. This can continue until you begin to sort out its impact on your life. There is a void that needs to be filled eventually, but you have no way to conceive of what your life will look like beyond that moment. You may feel lost and alone during this time even though you're surrounded by others.

> *"I was in denial for weeks. I examined what I can do and*
> *what I like to do. I wanted to switch to a different track*
> *of career. Then facing the reality of employability, I came*
> *back to the same track and started looking for a position*
> *similar to what I had been doing for three decades."*
> *– WJ, Engineer*

Feelings of anger can surface after the initial shock wears off. These feelings surface when you realize what has occurred and what its effect on you will be. It's important to recognize and deal with these feelings in a healthy way. The news is filled with headlines of disgruntled workers who direct their anger in violent ways. Accept your anger as part of the grieving process and channel the energy behind it accordingly. One exercise I frequently ask my clients to perform is to write a letter to the specific person or agency that terminated them. They are free to express themselves in any way they choose. They can use every strong expletive they ever learned, talk about their plan for revenge, or wish that the same would happen to them someday.

Once the person has written out their feelings of anger, they have two options. They can put the letter in an envelope and write the first name of a person on it with no other information, attach a stamp on it if they want, and then mail it. Or, they can hold a match to it and watch it burn before them. These are two forms of rituals for releasing any suppressed anger they are holding. The important part of this is to check in with your anger level before and after the ritual. Some clients have wanted to put specific mailing information on the envelope. My response is that this option is about letting go of the anger in order to move on, not to create a way to fuel it. If there is any residual anger present, it is time to write another letter and perform the same ritual on it. My clients have shared with me how effectively this works.

> *"I wish I would have done XXX instead.*
> *One door opens as another closes.*
> *I hated that job anyway. What will my friends say?*
> *How can I deal with this?"*
> – CW Technical Support Manager

In bargaining, the person seeks some rational explanation as to what occurred and plays out the options with a more desirable outcome resulting. These are the "if only" statements you play in your head. "If only I had been more observant of the red flags around the department shutdown." "If only I had been better at playing political football." "If only I had made myself more visible." While these types of statements might be helpful to future situations in the workplace, they will have zero effect on your status today.

Another emotion that accompanies loss is depression. This feeling is associated with the futility of the drive for control over the situation. The longer you're unemployed, the more likely you are to experience depression. It's more prevalent among middle-aged males and females and those who have worked in the blue-collar sector. It can become debilitating to the point that suicidal thoughts can occur. This is why it is important to stay connected to others during this time and to create a schedule that gives structure and direction to your life. It may be necessary to seek professional help to talk through your thoughts and feelings surrounding the changes in your life.

Once you take the steps needed to address your loss, you move into acceptance of the situation for what it is. I worked for a company for 22 years and thought that I would be there for years to come. That thought changed abruptly with a new administration. I left the position I had held and transferred to a lower level one. After grieving over the plan I had in mind, I accepted that I had a choice to focus on the past or move forward.

I chose the latter and became open to new options and opportunities. As I did this I felt a sense of empowerment. Not long after this, an offer for a position in an adjacent state which perfectly matched my background came across my desk. Eventually, I could see how this would not have occurred if I had fought to stay where I was.

Should you find yourself in the throes of either anger or depression while you're in job search mode, it's worth your while to work through those emotions, especially if you're preparing to interview. Imagine sitting across from your interviewer under their influence. Because over 90% of your communication is at a nonverbal level, the other person may be receiving signals that are contradictory to what you're saying with your words. This can be a function of your energy being affected by your depression. The listener may be internally asking, "Is this a person I would want to be working with on a daily basis?" Your anger may show up in your responses to how you dealt with problems in the workplace or when you're asked why you left your previous position. This is not the time for venting. You want to be at your best at this time, and your emotional state may sabotage the interview process.

It's not unusual to experience a sense of relief after the emotions related to a job loss have subsided. The conditions that existed in the workplace may look quite different after you're no longer employed there. There is a tendency to rationalize or minimize these conditions as a means of coping with a less than desirable situation. You may have been dealing with an overly demanding boss, an unrealistic work schedule, or lack of recognition for your efforts. For some individuals, the change in job status is seen as a blessing in disguise.

> *"Following my stunned shock over losing my job, I moved very quickly into an overwhelming state of euphoria. I had been incredibly unhappy in my job, so when it was over, I felt so much relief."*
> – JC, Director, Project Management

Exercise: Identify a time when you experienced a loss related to this area. What happened at the time? What actions did you take to deal with it? Describe your support system at the time of its occurrence. What did acceptance look like at the end of the experience?

Career

Nature of the loss: _______________________________________

____

____

Initial thoughts related to it: ___________________________

____

____

Initial feelings related to it: ___________________________

____

____

Actions taken during this time: ___________________________

____

____

Description of support system at this time: _______________

____

____

What did acceptance look like for you? ____________________

____

____

Affirmation:

I courageously face my losses during my job search, accepting that rejections and disappointments are a natural part of the job search process.

Identify stressors

*"The mind can go either direction under stress—
toward positive or toward negative: on or off.
Think of it as a spectrum whose extremes are
unconsciousness at the negative end and hyper
consciousness at the positive end. The way the mind
will lean under stress is strongly influenced by training."*
– Frank Herbert

Stress is the body's way of responding to a challenge. Your body releases specific chemicals designed to address that challenge. Epinephrine and cortisol are two of these chemicals present as hormones. They are the body's way of dealing with fight-or-flight events. Once the hormones are introduced into your body in reaction to the perceived threat, they eventually return to normal levels. But if the stress remains constant, the body cannot return to that state. It's at this time that stress-related conditions develop. Under the prolonged effects of these chemicals, you can develop hyperglycemia, high blood pressure, and a suppressed immunity system. The presence of these conditions is counterproductive in achieving your goals.

If you're in job search mode, stress is most likely a naturally occurring experience. There is the stress associated with what led to the change in employment status. This can be associated with what is referred to as the "bargaining" stage of dealing with loss. It's the stress created by replaying the circumstances that perhaps contributed to no longer being employed. "Maybe if I had worked harder and longer hours" or "Maybe if I had been willing to relocate even if it meant uprooting my family." It's as if an intervention of some kind on your part would have prevented this from happening. Creating this type of stress will not change the past and will only serve to keep you from moving forward. Ask yourself how this mental exercise will alter your present facts. If you want to use the bargaining stage productively, think about ways that you could address the circumstances you've identified in future positions.

Then there is the day-to-day stress that accompanies the actual job search once you begin it. "Where do I begin to look for a new job?" This is where having a plan is important. Map out your job search strategies much as you would plan for a trip. Where you are today is your starting point. Your destination is your next position. What route will you travel to get from Point A to Point B? Who will you choose as your navigator and crew to help get you there? How will you handle roadblocks and detours along the way? Having a plan will help to reduce your stress levels.

Next comes the preparation for the job that you believe matches who you are and what you have to offer. "How do I fill in the boxes on the application so that I don't eliminate myself before I even get an interview?" "What should I include and not include on my resume?" "How should I prepare for my upcoming interview?" Think of who and what your resources are and take advantage of them. Use online resources as well as colleagues and professionals who can help guide you through this phase of the job search.

Regardless of whether you're looking for work or are currently employed, it's critical that you be aware of what the contributors to your stress are. The workplace is a common source of stress these days. "Will the job I have today be there tomorrow?" "How do I keep up with the demands of the job now that there are fewer of us left to do the work?" "How do I deal with coworkers who don't do their fair share of the workload?" "My boss makes unreasonable demands upon me. What can I do about that?" As these questions weigh on your mind, your body is supplying the hormones in reaction to them. One effect of this physiological state is reduced cognitive functioning. Being stressed doesn't improve your problem-solving abilities. Create a list of the stressors present and then rank them in the order of their effect on your life.

Possible stressors can include:

Apathy - Do you find yourself losing interest in the work you do? Does the work you do no longer provide satisfaction and enjoyment? If you're looking for work, do you find yourself not really caring if you find employment? Do you find yourself arriving at work just when you are scheduled to begin and leaving as soon as you have put in your hours? Has work become a way to fill in the hours of your day?

Changes in employment practices - Has your company shifted from primarily full-time workers to contract workers? Has there been a shift to outsourcing as a way to save the company money? Have the job duties of those employees who have left been transferred to those remaining without a plan to hire new workers to assume their duties?

Family - Are there any recent changes to your relationships, i.e. have you recently married or decided to move in with a significant other? Are you covering living expenses for another person including a spouse, a child, or a relative? Are you covering the educational expenses for at least one child? Are you contributing to your parents' living expenses that they are unable to cover themselves?

Health - Are you facing a change in health that affects your ability to perform your job duties and life tasks in general? Are you finding it more difficult to perform physical tasks that used to be effortless for you? Have you noticed changes in your ability to maintain your focus or remember new procedures? Are you gaining weight because of the sedentary nature of the work you do?

Life pressures - Do you compare yourself to others and question why you aren't where they are? Do you find yourself falling further behind in the skills needed to perform your job duties? Do you avoid people thinking that they will ask you about your progress in your current job search? Do you question your purpose in life asking, "What am I doing here?"

Money - Would you consider yourself to be a saver or a spender? Do you have a plan for dealing with a job loss or a major expenditure such as a home or car repair? Do you never seem to have enough month at the end of your paycheck? How do the increases in your pay reflect the change in cost of living? How many sources of income do you have? If you're currently searching for work, how have you planned to cover expenses until you're hired in your next position? Are you receiving unemployment benefits? How long before they expire?

Rejection - Have you had interviews scheduled with no job offer following them? Have you been told you're overqualified or underqualified and therefore are not being considered as a candidate for the position? Have you applied for a promotion at work and been passed over for it? Do you question your age, ethnicity, or gender as affecting your consideration for being hired?

Routine - Are you comfortable with changes in routine and structure? Do you find that routine and structure are important to you in providing consistency? Do you spend hours watching video games or television wondering where the time has gone and accomplishing little?

Time constraints - How are you able to pace yourself to meet deadlines in your current position? Do you feel like you're juggling four balls in the air with no relief in sight? Are you constantly having to deal with interruptions and unexpected problems that distract you and those you work with from maintaining your focus?

Uncertainty - Do you ever wonder if anyone cares or notices what you contribute at work? Do you hear other employees talking about the possibilities of layoffs or outsourcing? Do you ever ask yourself if the work you're currently doing is still right for you and if there is any future in it for you? If you're unemployed, do you ask yourself how long it will be before you're hired?

Once you have identified the source of your stress, the next step is to identify ways to reduce or postpone the cause. Let's say that one source of stress for you is feeling like you're having to take on more than your share of the workload. Write down several recent examples of how that has occurred and who the individuals are that are not doing their part. Now ask yourself what actions you could take to remediate that problem. Would talking to each of them personally help to understand what may be preventing them from contributing to the tasks needed to get the work done? If so, how can you do this without accusing or blaming? This approach to stress creates a sense of empowerment. You move from feeling helpless and put upon to taking responsibility for your part in the matter and taking positive action to address it.

Exercise: Given the list of possible stressors listed above, how would you rate yourself overall within each of them on a scale of 1 (Low) - 10 (High)? Place an X along the continuum that corresponds to that rating.

Apathy

| 1 | 2 | 3 | 4 | 5 | 6 | 7 | 8 | 9 | 10 |

Changes in employment practices

| 1 | 2 | 3 | 4 | 5 | 6 | 7 | 8 | 9 | 10 |

Family

| 1 | 2 | 3 | 4 | 5 | 6 | 7 | 8 | 9 | 10 |

Health

| 1 | 2 | 3 | 4 | 5 | 6 | 7 | 8 | 9 | 10 |

Life pressures

| 1 | 2 | 3 | 4 | 5 | 6 | 7 | 8 | 9 | 10 |

Money

| 1 | 2 | 3 | 4 | 5 | 6 | 7 | 8 | 9 | 10 |

Rejection

| 1 | 2 | 3 | 4 | 5 | 6 | 7 | 8 | 9 | 10 |

Routine

| 1 | 2 | 3 | 4 | 5 | 6 | 7 | 8 | 9 | 10 |

Time Constraints

| 1 | 2 | 3 | 4 | 5 | 6 | 7 | 8 | 9 | 10 |

Uncertainty

| 1 | 2 | 3 | 4 | 5 | 6 | 7 | 8 | 9 | 10 |

Other (specify) _______________

| 1 | 2 | 3 | 4 | 5 | 6 | 7 | 8 | 9 | 10 |

For any area that you rated higher than a 3, what actions can you take to decrease that number? Record those actions in the chart on the following page.

Area	Actions	Initial start date	Follow-up date	Follow-up date	Follow-up date	Follow-up date

Area	Actions	Initial start date	Follow-up date	Follow-up date	Follow-up date	Follow-up date

Set up a system for tracking your actions to determine their effectiveness in decreasing your stress levels in each of the areas identified. At the end of a specified time, revisit the area and rate yourself on your level. Determine if you will continue the actions you have identified to either maintain or reduce your stress levels further. Then set the next date to check in on your progress. Feel free to revise your actions based on their effectiveness.

Remind yourself that nothing is forever. Ask yourself if you could live with the stressor today if you knew that it's temporary. Deadlines are one example of sources of temporary stress. There are some individuals who thrive on the increased pressure of knowing that a project is due tomorrow. Somehow it stimulates their creative juices and they are able to create a product that appears to have been weeks in the making. Their bodies are still producing those chemicals that can contribute to physical ailments in the future. The question then becomes, "What are they doing to reduce that effect during the time that they are focusing all of their energy on the project?" Then there are those individuals who are able to pace themselves so that the stress on them is minimized. They allow themselves enough time to address any unforeseen events that could affect completion of the project so it can be delivered on time.

When you're experiencing stress there are a number of ways to reduce its effect on you. One way is to learn to relax. Stress has a direct effect on your muscles and organs. Relaxation techniques can help slow your heart rate, reduce the need for oxygen thus increasing the flow of blood to your muscles, and reduce your blood pressure. While we typically think of relaxation as any activity that is separate from your daily routine, this may not be enough to prompt a physiological change. You want to consciously interrupt the train of thought to decrease the activity of the sympathetic nervous system. You can accomplish this state through practices such as meditation and yoga.

If you choose to meditate, realize that it will take practice and discipline. The challenge is to slow down the mind chatter. It isn't until you begin to delve into this method of relaxing that you become aware of the constant self-talk that is generated in your mind. As a novice to meditation, I became aware that within a few seconds my thoughts were racing ahead to what I needed to do next or on some completely unrelated subject. When this would occur I would notice it, acknowledge it, and then bring my focus back to the meditation. This is not the time to be judging yourself on your ability to learn this discipline. The more you do this, the better you will become at developing mastery of the technique.

You may decide that you would benefit more from using a guided meditation. This form of meditation involves listening to a prerecorded format that generally includes calming background music and a structure that keeps you focused. Commit to keeping with it for a month for you to observe progress. Remind yourself of what you were sensing in your body when you first began and what that is like four weeks later. There should be a noticeable difference in your heart rate, your breathing, and your sense of wellbeing. All of these are measures of stress levels and should continue to be positively influenced by a conscious daily habit of meditation.

There is no one right approach to meditation. Thousands of techniques have been developed over time. There appear to be five general categories of meditation, and it's important to identify the one that works most effectively for you. One technique is referred to as a concentration meditation. It's the one that we most often associate with meditation. It involves learning how to sustain a mental focus without distraction. It was easiest for me to use an object, such as a candle, to provide that focus. I would use a dark room, free of background noise, and stare at the flame, shutting out any competing thoughts. Over time, I expanded my ability to do this from a few seconds to about 20 minutes.

Another category of meditational techniques is called mindfulness meditation. This type of meditation occurs when you're completely absorbed in an experience such as a sunset, a night sky, a rainbow, or a snowfall. It opens you up to a sense of wonder and appreciation as each moment unfolds. One such experience occurred for me while I was attending an event on a mountaintop in Oregon one summer. On a day filled with while billowy clouds, I looked up into the sky and observed the sun reflecting off of ice droplets projecting rainbows onto the surface of the clouds. I was fixated on the phenomenon and found myself feeling awe and wonder at its presence.

There are several other categories of meditation. Reflective meditation centers on a specific question or topic you pose requiring that you focus your attention on the topic allowing answers to follow. Creative meditation is a way to actively nurture positive characteristics by visualizing them present within you. Finally, the category of heart-centered meditation techniques opens you to compassion for all living things. None of the techniques are mutually exclusive of one another. All that matters is that you find the technique that works for you.

Another method for reducing stress is yoga. The purpose of yoga is to create strength, harmony, and awareness in both the mind and body through breathing, meditation, and established postures. In addition to its physical benefits, yoga contributes to stress reduction by relaxing the mind and sharpening concentration. There are over 100 schools or types of yoga so it's important to find the one that best suits your needs.

While meditation and yoga are found to be highly effective in altering your thought processes leading to a reduction in stress levels, there are other ways that people have found to meet this goal. Listening to relaxing music, taking a 20-minute walk, soaking in a warm tub, gardening, vigorous exercise, and watching a romantic comedy can also make a difference for you. Once you have identified those that you enjoy, make a commitment to incorporate them into your daily routine. You can monitor the effects of your activities in several ways. You can track your blood pressure, number of hours you're sleeping, and your energy levels. One of the benefits of using these stress reducers is that you can build a healthier immune system. Prior to Covid-19, I traveled all over the world and did not catch anything from my fellow passengers, even during the height of the cold and flu season. Think about the frequency of your days spent in bed due to sickness and consider how they may be related to your body's reaction to stress. See if that changes after adopting a stress reduction program.

Affirmation:

I take inventory of the external factors that may be sources of stress, reminding myself that I have the inner resources and resilience to navigate through them.

Seek emotional support

*"Too often we underestimate the power of a touch,
a smile, a kind word, a listening ear,
an honest compliment, or the smallest act of caring,
all of which have the potential to turn a life around."*
− Leo Buscaglia

There is the type of support you need when you're focused on achieving a goal such as finding a new position. This involves making a plan and working with others to fine tune it and adding the element of accountability. Then there is the emotional component of transition. This requires a different level of support during those times when you're struggling to accept who you are and what you're going through. This is the time when you feel overwhelmed, depressed, angry, or worthless. You may be chided with, "Stop feeling sorry for yourself. There are a lot of people who are worse off than you." Or, "Maybe you just aren't trying hard enough." The person telling you this may have good intentions, but this is not what you need to hear to survive these emotional bouts. This is the time when you would benefit from talking to others who can identify with what you're experiencing. Recall how you have felt after sharing your situation with another person who is not there to judge or *fix* you. **Sometimes all you need is an empathetic ear from someone who has been in your shoes.**

When choosing a support group related to a job loss, think about what you hope to gain by joining them. Look for opportunities to connect with others who not only understand what you're going through but also can help to provide structure and direction. If you're seeking a group of people to listen to you vent from one session to the next, ask yourself how you will improve your situation by doing so. Venting may initially feel good, as it's a way to release toxic thinking, but you may find yourself replaying those toxic scenarios over and over without any progress being made. Look at your goal as living the image you create as you overcome what brought you to a particular group to begin with. It may be related to weight loss, the desire to stop smoking or drinking, or dealing with a job loss.

After leaving my 34-year career in education, I thought that finding my next job would be rather simple. Within two months of leaving, I experienced what I had warned others might happen next. The stress that I had bottled up within me that led to my decision to submit my resignation showed up in physical form. I spent a month in bed with what was to be diagnosed as pneumonia. Any desire to look for work was curtailed by a cough that jarred my body from head to toe, and I had little energy for doing even basic tasks. It's not unusual for our stored emotions and stress to release themselves in this manner. Once I recovered I was ready to explore new options.

Following my bout with pneumonia, a friend told me about a group of professionals who were unemployed and working together to support one another through these challenging times. I signed up to become a part of the group with no idea of what it would be like or what it might lead to. The most appropriate word to describe how I felt those first few weeks I attended the program was "numb." The world I had known was behind me, and I did not have the capacity to project into a sunny future. What I did have was the willingness to trust that this could work. As the weeks passed my self-confidence began to grow. I tapped into skills that I had rarely used like answering the telephone and providing information to others seeking assistance. I also explored renewing my focus on career coaching through volunteer work with my fellow job seekers.

It gave me a renewed sense of hope and a path to consider. By following the structure they provided, I was taking the steps to the work I am doing today. Years later, I am still in contact with some of the people I met within that group.

Find a group that matches your interests and goals. Take time to get to know people within the group. You can do this by observing the dynamics of how people interact. In some cases, there are established ground rules that guide the acceptability of behaviors by its members. These are generally related to mutual respect for each other by suspending judgment, allowing everyone present with an opportunity to speak, as well as not pressuring someone who is not comfortable sharing their thoughts. If there are assigned leaders, what do they do to facilitate participation? Are there individuals who tend to dominate discussions while the majority of those attending remain silent? Do you feel welcomed by those in the group? If you discover that the group does not meet your needs and there is no way for you to change that, seek out another group. You don't need to add to your stress by trying to be a square peg in a round hole.

Another course of action is to work with a professional to address the feelings you're having at this time. This is generally a counselor or therapist who can work with you to identify alternative ways to deal with situations in your life. The counselor or therapist helps to explore the thought processes that may be blocking you from moving forward in your life and assist in identifying more productive ways to cope with life's challenges. This can occur in either an individual or group setting. An advantage of the

> "[I am] joining success teams that comprise of others looking for a job."
> – Claire R, Manager, Customer Solutions

group setting is that it allows you to practice new behaviors in a supportive environment. Constructive feedback can be provided by both the counselor or therapist as well as group members. The goal is to have you become confident enough with these new behaviors to practice them in public.

When considering using the services of such a professional, it's helpful to speak to them about their approach to working with clients. There are a number of schools of thought on how services are to be delivered. Ask the person to explain to you how they would work with you. Having been educated as a counselor, I was exposed to many different approaches and theories. Each of them has a specific way of addressing presenting problems. Find out how they determine when the client has been successful in achieving their goals and how they work with you to do that.

Exercise: List three potential groups for providing emotional and professional support. Next to them list a brief description of the services provided and their contact information.

Name of group	Services provided	Contact information

Name of group	Services provided	Contact information

Decide how you plan to participate in this group.

Are you looking for regularly scheduled meetings?   YES __ NO __

Do you prefer face-to-face, online, or a combination of both types of participation? _______

How far are you willing to travel to attend face-to-face meetings? _______ miles

What is the earliest date you can begin participation based on your contact with the group? _______

What arrangements might you need to make to participate (childcare, transportation, etc.) and how would you cover that?____

What date are you setting to participate for your first time? _______

Affirmation:

I am open to seeking and receiving emotional support during my job search, sharing my fears and triumphs with those I trust.

Say your goodbyes

*"Farewell has a sweet sound of reluctance.
Goodbye is short and final, a word with teeth sharp
to bite through the string that ties past to the future."*
– John Steinbeck

Sometimes the hardest part of making a transition to the future is having to say goodbye to the past. What was familiar is no more. You're saying goodbye to the people and experiences that helped shape your life and brought you to where you are today. This is why we so often attach rituals to our endings. We hold graduation ceremonies, arrange farewell parties when people leave their current place of employment or relocate, and celebrate the end of the current year and look forward with hope and anticipation as the new one arrives. Sometimes you maintain the relationships that were formed, but most often they pass away with time unless there is a way to keep them current. People who I thought would be in my life forever have moved on in their lives, as have I. I knew when it was time to say goodbye to that relationship to open myself up to new ones.

Goodbyes help provide closure. When I would leave a job or prepare to move, the last gesture on my part was to turn and say goodbye to its presence. In some cases, there was a deep sense of emotion in the form of sorrow, especially if the majority of my experiences there were positive. But often there was a sense of relief as I accepted that it was time to move on. It didn't seem to matter how long my stay had been. It was more about the memories attached to that stay. When I started up my car to move across the country in my late 20s, I spent about half an hour in tears. It wasn't about the almost two years I had lived in my apartment, but about the almost 30 years of friends and family that was about to change. As a new life unfolded before me, the pain of separation lessened to be replaced by the excitement of a new chapter in my life.

> *"I quit my job because I was so stressed out. I felt relieved, free, sad that I was letting go of not only my income, which caused a new stress, but that I wouldn't see people I liked anymore."*
> – AL

When you're making a transition, think of ways to make your goodbyes. If you're someone who needs to have personal interaction with others as a part of that process, plan a get-together with significant people to share what meeting them has meant to you. If this is not something you're comfortable with, plan one-on-one time, especially if you know that it will involve a heavy expression of emotions. Focus on sharing what was positive. This is what people will remember most of your last time together. If there is a sense of bitterness or regret as you leave, take time for introspection as to what your unfinished business is and work toward its resolution. If there is a particular person that you're holding a grudge against, you may want to reserve your goodbyes to him or her until you're in a stronger place. It's more important that you part with dignity than a confrontation.

Exercise: Write how you said goodbye to your former job. Did you have any type of event at work to acknowledge your departure? What was that like for you? If you did not have an event, how did you gain closure on the experience? Are there any goodbyes that need to be made so that you can move on? With whom would they be and how could you do that in a productive manner?

Affirmation:

I release any attachments to the past, knowing that each goodbye is an opportunity for growth and new beginnings.

Key Learning Points

- A change in status is often accompanied by feelings of loss.
- Stress can have counterproductive effects, physiologically, mentally, and emotionally.
- Transition involves dealing with a multitude of emotional responses.
- To move forward it's necessary to have closure on what was left behind.

What is your story around acceptance as you read through this chapter? What was it that triggered your thoughts around this?

CHAPTER FIVE

Resilience

"The oak fought the wind and was broken;
the willow bent when it must and survived.
– Robert Jordan

Resilience self-assessment quiz

Mark **Yes** or **No** as it applies to your life today.

1. I know how to care for my basic needs.	Yes	No
2. I know that there is a purpose and a meaning to my life.	Yes	No
3. I can recall challenging experiences in my life and what I did to get through them.	Yes	No
4. I believe that working through challenges will make me stronger.	Yes	No
5. I can name at least three people I could talk to about a problem.	Yes	No
6. I take the time I need to evaluate a setback and then move forward with my new plan.	Yes	No
7. I know when I am feeling overwhelmed and what I can do about it.	Yes	No
8. I respond rather than react to crises.	Yes	No
9. I can see the humor in life's challenges.	Yes	No
10. I consider myself to be adaptable to changes around me.	Yes	No

To determine your score, count the number of **Yes** statements. ____

8-10 You indicate a **high** degree of ability within this area.

4-7 You indicate a **moderate** degree of ability within this area.

1-3 You indicate a **low** degree of ability within this area.

Resilience defined

When you're struggling with a transition think back to a similar time in your life. It may have been a move to a new location, a change in jobs, ending a relationship, or a financial crisis. Recall the circumstances surrounding that change for you. As you experienced an end to what was happening, what feelings and thoughts accompanied that for you? Did you wonder at the time if life would ever return to normal and how long it would be before that happened? What did you do between the time one situation ended and a new one took over your attention? How did it feel once you began to live life from that new perspective? Your ability to recover from an unfortunate circumstance or illness is what we refer to as *resilience*.

Do you know someone who seems capable of handling adversity in a healthy manner? It doesn't mean that they have adopted a Pollyanna attitude where they paste a smile on their face as if nothing seems to affect them, but rather they recognize the severity of the situation and face it head-on. They see it as it is and ask themselves what they can do about it. They see the world less as negatively doing something to them and more as how they positively function in the world. They are realistic in what they can and cannot change. Some people believe that resilience is limited to a select few, but it can be acquired by most who recognize its benefits. Resilience is the product of how you interact with your environment. When dealing with difficulties such as a job loss, how quickly can you assess its impact on you and take measures to regain control of your life?

> *"I thought that I would be more resilient than I actually
> was and that I would start my job search right away."*
> –TH, Program Manager

Think of your overall attitude toward life. Do you view the world as a place that is filled with one challenge after another that never gives you time to recover or a world filled with opportunities for growth? Imagine going through life being hypervigilant of the dangers that might befall you. The bottom line is that no one is immune to events such as the death of a loved one, financial crises, or losing a job. At some point, you will be faced with any or all of them. Will you experience pain and sorrow upon their arrival? Most likely. If you focus on resilience your recovery time will be much shorter. There appears to be a correlation between the cultivation of positive emotions and resilience. One of these emotions you will often hear mentioned during times of duress is hope. In the ancient Greek myth of Pandora's Box, this was the only entity that remained after all of the ills of the world had been released.

Meet your basic needs

> *"Everybody needs beauty as well as bread,*
> *places to play in and pray in where nature may heal and*
> *cheer and give strength to the body and soul."*
> – John Muir

It's difficult to be resilient when your physical and emotional needs are not being met. American psychologist, Abraham Maslow, described a hierarchy of needs that begin with satisfying your physiological needs for food, clothing, and shelter. As each level of needs is met, it allows the individual to seek the next higher one culminating in self-actualization. Think about the amount of energy it takes to survive when your only thoughts are focused on finding enough food and water to get you through the day. This can be a serious problem for an individual who can barely scrape up enough money to cover such expenses. When you're unemployed, the resources needed for survival may be limited. There may be times when it's necessary to put pride aside and accept what others have to share. We live in a society that emphasizes success based on our material possessions. When you're not working, access to those items may be compromised. It helps to differentiate what you need from what you want. Take time to list what you have and in which of these two categories it would be placed.

> *"Taking time to heal. Don't think of anything work-related for a while. Focus on other neglected aspects of life."*
> – MW, Project manager

During times of change, there can be a shift in what is most important to you based on your financial resources. Your need to cover your rent or mortgage to keep a roof over your head supersedes the purchase of a new car or the latest technological gadget. Your habit of eating out at a restaurant two or three times per week is replaced by having your meals primarily at home. You decide that buying that new sweater or shoes can be put on hold and that what you have in your closet will work for now. All of these are ways that you adapt to your current status. It also serves as motivation for pursuing options for meeting those needs, allowing you to seek higher aspirations. While there may be a temptation to spend money on something frivolous, refer to the list of wants and needs you created and remind yourself that the want can be satisfied once your income increases. Look for inexpensive ways to treat yourself, like a nature walk or attending a free concert.

It's also important to address your emotional needs at this time. One of our greatest emotional needs relates to security. This is a sense of safety that is innate to how you see yourself growing. When you have internalized that sense of safety, you can open yourself up to risk. You understand your limitations and work within that framework. As you become comfortable with the behaviors that accompany this new view of who you are there will be a natural tendency to stretch yourself further. Having a healthy sense of security shows up as confidence in who you are and what you have to offer. This is quite the opposite from someone who acts out of their insecurities by blaming others and pointing out their imperfections.

Another emotional need is that of giving and receiving attention. Think of a time when you felt invisible. This can translate into thoughts that your presence doesn't matter. In the workplace, this can play itself out during downsizing and offshoring. When asked what is most important to employees, employers will often cite adequate financial compensation. If you ask the same question of employees, they will express a need to be recognized for their work. Ask yourself when was the last time that you received acknowledgment for a task you had performed. How did you feel when you were told either privately or publicly that your presence made a difference? Now think about the times when your work went unnoticed. How did that feel? During my work for an agency for almost two years, I received no feedback from those above me on how effectively I was performing my duties. Unless you have a strong internal sense of accomplishment, you're left wondering about the value of your work. This can have a negative impact on your motivation. While it's important to be the recipient of attention and recognition, it's just as critical to deliver it. How do you typically let others know that they are doing well? Do you offer words of encouragement, suggestions to make their lives easier, or praise to their supervisor?

While there is any number of emotional needs that contribute to resilience, a sense of belonging is perhaps one of the most important to consider. Each of us has an inherent need to belong to something greater than ourselves. This can be a family, a circle of friends, co-workers, affiliation with a group such as a team, political party, or charitable organization, or as encompassing as the citizenry of a country. Belonging to a group provides you with a sense of identity and affiliation. Think about a time when you made a significant change in some area of your life. Perhaps you moved across the state or country to attend school or start a new job. Your previous social ties were broken in that you no longer had face-to-face interactions with people you considered to be important. You began to seek out those who most matched what you had left. You explored settings where you could forge new relationships. Eventually, you developed bonds that provided you with support and attachment. These were the people you could count on to understand you because they shared your experiences and preferences.

Exercise: Next to each statement rate yourself as to where you are today. This may take some introspection, and it will provide you with a sense of where you need to be headed to change that. Place the date in the corresponding box so that you can monitor your progress as you take action to address it. Each time you review it, place that date in the box.

Physical Needs:	Low	Medium	High
Ability to provide sufficient **food** for self and family			
Ability to provide appropriate **clothing** for self and family			
Ability to provide adequate **shelter** for self and family			
Ability to provide proper **transportation** for self and family			
Ability to provide adequate **medical coverage** for self and family			

For any area that you marked Low, what resources do you have to increase that to at least a Medium?

____

____

What actions steps will you take based upon this information?

____

____

Emotional Needs:	Low	Medium	High
Security			
Attention			
Control			
Connectedness			
Friendship			
Privacy			
Belonging			

Emotional Needs:	Low	Medium	High
Competence			
Meaning and Purpose			

For any area that you marked Low, what resources do you have to increase that to at least a Medium?

____

____

What actions steps will you take based upon this information?

____

____

For many individuals, the workplace becomes a natural environment for forming social bonds. Consider the amount of time you spend interacting with co-workers. If you're working full time you're spending a third of your day in their presence. You discuss your challenges with your job, issues you may be dealing with related to your boss, as well as the ups and downs that come with working alongside others. You may develop deep friendships with others in your company, and they will be the ones you may likely turn to when problems arise because of their knowledge of the key players involved. Talking to them can shed new light on a situation, especially when it comes to office politics, and is typically used as a way to build alliances. When faced with negative circumstances, these individuals can offer support and suggest options to help you survive emotionally. They do so with the belief that you will do the same should they encounter problems themselves.

At the same time, it's important to recognize that everyone you work with may not have your back. You may encounter individuals with a hidden agenda in garnering your trust. Sharing details of personal and professional problems with co-workers may result in a face-to-face meeting with your superiors, so think about the content and intent of your confiding before you do so. In this case, discernment may save your job and reputation, especially when you're unaware of where the true alliances reside.

While workplace bonds are a natural occurrence, imagine what it's like when that resource is no longer available because your position has been terminated. There can be a feeling of loss and loneliness that follows. Your support system has been critically altered. Even if you're able to continue your relationship with former coworkers, the strength of the dynamics begins to erode because you're no longer an active participant within their environment. New employees, supervisors, and customers come on stage in your absence, and what was once familiar becomes more foreign. Now what you hear are secondhand reports that lack a personal connection. Moving on requires that you look for new ways to belong outside of your old place of employment.

Look for new opportunities to share what you're going through to identify steps you can take to change your current status. One way this can be accomplished is through membership in professional organizations. Here you will find people who understand the changes that are taking place within your field and offer direction and resources. You're also less likely to become a victim of office politics since members of professional organizations are unlikely to be employed by the same company. This can be valuable when your emotional state is vulnerable.

Ask yourself what it is that you need from those around you while you are in transition. You may need information, money, support, or time. Who do you know who can most likely provide that to you? Are you willing to reach out to ask for what you need? If not, consider what it is that keeps you from doing so. Usually, it's some type of fear. Perhaps you're choosing to reject yourself and your needs before anyone else can. The worst that can happen is that the person is either unable or unwilling to help. If they can't offer a suggestion as to other resources, thank them and move on to the next person. One of the most effective sales strategies is to ask for the sale as a way to close the deal. It may take asking as many as ten people before you get a "Yes." Eventually, you will connect to the right person who can provide that "Yes."

To track how you're doing in meeting your basic needs, write five of them down on a small card that you can easily carry in your wallet or pocket. Take the list out during the day and place a check next to any of the needs that you have attended to since the last time you looked at it. It will let you know which ones are being maintained and which ones might need more attention. You might notice patterns and consciously plan to address that need.

Affirmation:

I prioritize meeting my basic needs during my job search, acknowledging that taking care of myself is essential for navigating this journey with resilience and clarity.

Capitalize on strengths and abilities

"I know and you know that you have more energy, strength, power, and awareness than you can imagine; nothing or nobody can stop you from achieving whatever you desire but you and your self-belief. So focus on your belief in your ability, your skill, and yourself."
– Ricardo Housham

Every human being is endowed with strengths and abilities that set them apart from everyone who has lived or will live on this planet. Two people may possess the ability to professionally play the piano, but there will be subtle differences in their performance of a piece. Two people may demonstrate strong verbal presentation skills, but their delivery style can be very unlike one another. It's your responsibility to identify and develop those strengths and abilities through the work you do and the life you lead. Should you find yourself between jobs, use the time to take inventory of what you do well. There are countless free online assessments that can provide that information if you're unsure of what your strengths are.

Once you have compiled a list of your strengths and abilities, rate them on a scale of 1 (low) to 5 (high) as to your confidence level in using them. For those items that scored less than 5, ask yourself what holds you back from expressing them as fully as those you rated as a 5. If you have any doubts about how well you do in the lower scoring items, write an account of your success in the past with them. As you do so, you will likely uncover more strengths and abilities that you hadn't even thought of.

One activity I assign to my clients is to have them list what are referred to as natural talents. These are behaviors that you engage in with little or no effort. You may have a natural talent for playing a tune by ear, constructing furniture, or solving an algebra problem. You wonder why everyone else can't do it as easily as you do. As you go through your day, think about the various tasks you perform and which ones come naturally for you. Natural talents are not to be confused with habits that are performed with little effort based on constant repetition. Driving your car, making your bed, or saving a word document on your computer are examples of behaviors that are performed repetitively. If you aren't sure what your natural talents are, just ask someone who knows you to point out what they see you do that they wish they could do as easily.

Exercise: List five of your natural talents. Next to each of them provide an example of how you use them in your life.

Natural Talents	How I use them

Once you're clear on what your strengths and talents are, look for ways to express them on a regular basis. They are like muscles that benefit from daily use; otherwise, they atrophy. Sometimes they require a concerted effort to develop and maintain. If you have strengths in the area of mathematics, they won't increase if you only use what you currently know. Think of ways to challenge your current base of information. How could you take that information to the next level? Would it mean pursuing advanced coursework or seeking opportunities to apply what you know to solve a work-related problem? We know that the brain is much more plastic and adaptable than we had believed in the past. Acknowledge the work that you do to grow as a way to build your self-confidence and self-esteem.

Affirmation:

I confidently capitalize on my strengths and abilities during my job search, communicating my strengths with clarity and conviction, allowing me to articulate the value I can bring to potential employers.

Develop problem-solving and communication skills

"A key to healthy problem solving is good communication."
– Asa Don Brown

A problem consists of a situation that requires an action to either change or maintain what is happening at the moment. The change could involve something as minor as needing more light in a room to perform a task or finding a misplaced set of keys. Or it could be a major one such as developing a vaccine for a debilitating disease or reducing the incidence of hunger in the world. An action to maintain a situation might involve keeping someone alive who has just sustained life-threatening injuries. Each scenario is likely subject to multiple solutions. The solution is the achievement of a desired goal that provides the best answer for the situation at hand at that moment.

One statement that is overly used when individuals or teams are attempting to solve a problem is, "That will never work." With those four words, the momentum that has been driving the project forward can come to a screeching halt. Further suggestions and ideas are more reluctantly shared for fear of criticism and judgment. This can be particularly true when you're in the process of finding new employment and are testing uncharted waters.

You may share your thoughts about starting your own business or changing fields. You might want to begin such conversations with, "I was thinking about an option that I might pursue and I wanted to run it by you. I'd appreciate any ideas that you might have that would be important for me to consider to research." This approach leads the discussion into what we call "open-ended" responses as opposed to "closed-ended" ones. Closed-ended responses elicit a one-word reaction such as "Yes" or "No" that terminate the question. It could sound like, "Do you think I would be wise to start my own business?" You don't acquire much more information beyond their one-word answer. Practice beginning your requests with "What," "Why'" and "How" to elicit the information you need.

There are many people who benefit from externalizing their thoughts or what we call "thinking out loud." I am one such person and have found this method of communicating my thoughts to be misunderstood by others. They have interpreted my externalized thoughts as statements of intent. Later they would ask why I hadn't taken action on my words to complete a task. When I explained that this was just thinking aloud, I was chastised not to do that again. I still think out loud, but preface my statements as such. It has made life easier for everyone. Think about how you communicate when dealing with a problem and make sure that your listeners are clear on what you're saying so that it's not confused with a commitment.

When discussing your problem, stay focused on the present and the future. Talk about what you can be doing today to affect your future. Refer to the past when it comes to what you have learned from it. You will not resolve a problem if you use this time to complain or vent about past hurts or affronts. If you find yourself engaging in this type of talk, make a mental note of it and deal with it later. Otherwise, it will cast a shadow over your conversation and alter what you hear. Remind yourself that there is little you can do to change the past, so why dwell on it.

Exercise: Identify a specific problem you're having. Now read it over and decide if you have enough information to solve it. If the answer is No, what information do you need and how would you go about collecting it? What are possible solutions to the problem? Which solution appears to work best to address the problem? What actions do you need to take to achieve the solution?

Specific problem: ____

Current information: ____

____

____

____

Additional information needed: ___________________________________

____

____

____

Plan for gathering additional information: _________________________

____

____

____

List several possible solutions below. Circle the number next to the solution that best addresses the problem.

1. ____

2. ____

3. ____

4. ____

5. ____

6. ____

Place a #1 next to the solution that best addresses the problem. Actions needed:

1. ____

2. ____

3. ____

4. ____

5. ____

The key element to effectively solving problems is active listening. Listen to understand the other person's point of view. I often take notes when the other person is speaking, especially if I know there is going to be extensive information provided. I will interject questions and paraphrase what I have heard to clarify content. Paraphrasing is a helpful tool in communicating since it allows you to capture and summarize the speaker's words. Using statements such as "Let me make sure I understand what you're saying," and "Tell me more about what you just said" will reduce the likelihood of misunderstanding. Thank the person for sharing their thoughts and give yourself time to reflect upon what they have told you. This will give you the time you need to evaluate their ideas and determine the next steps.

Exercise: Practice your paraphrasing skills by talking to five different people. Ask them to respond to the following request, "Tell me about a time when you felt successful." Use the space below to capture the key points of their response. When each person has completed their story, write your paraphrasing response in no more than three sentences. Then read it aloud to the person for your accuracy in capturing their intention. If you inaccurately report a point, seek clarification with, "Let me make sure I understand this." Finally, look for areas of improvement based on the feedback you receive from the other person.

Person 1:

Key points of Story:

____

____

Your paraphrasing:

____

____

Points of clarification needed:

____

____

Areas of improvement needed:

____

____

Person 2:

Key points of Story:

____

____

Your paraphrasing:

____

____

Points of clarification needed:

____

____

Areas of improvement needed:

____

____

Person 3:

Key points of Story:

____

____

Your paraphrasing:

____

____

Points of clarification needed:

____

____

Areas of improvement needed:

____

____

Person 4:

Key points of Story:

____

____

Your paraphrasing:

____

____

Points of clarification needed:

____

____

Areas of improvement needed:

____

____

Person 5:

Key points of Story:

____

____

Your paraphrasing:

____

____

Points of clarification needed:

____

____

Areas of improvement needed:

____

____

Affirmation:

I am committed to developing my problem-solving and communication skills during my job search, embracing feedback as a valuable tool for growth, welcoming constructive criticism, and using it to refine my problem-solving and communication abilities.

Challenge negative messages

> *"He who would be useful, strong, and happy must cease to be a passive receptacle for the negative, beggarly, and impure streams of thought; and as a wise householder commands his servants and invites his guests, so must he learn to command his desires and to say, with authority, what thoughts he shall admit into the mansion of his soul."*
> – James Allen

When you're going through a transition, there will be times when negative messages will surface from both yourself and others. These messages can consist of predictions and judgments of what could occur in the future. Self-talk might sound like "I'll never find a decent paying job again. There's no hope for me." "Looks like I'm ending up just like my father (or mother) said I would—a failure." "I did everything I was told and look how it ended." From the perspective of others it might sound like "See what happens when you follow your dreams. You should have chosen a career that had a solid future." "What were you thinking when you passed up that promotion because you had to move across the country?" "Just take the next job that comes along and be glad you have one."

Without a strong sense of self-worth, these thoughts and statements can plant seeds of doubt as to your ability to change your future. They will keep you from taking the steps needed to pursue your dreams or break a pattern that is leading to a dead end. This can be paralyzing and serves little, if any, purpose in taking positive action. Should you find yourself listening to and accepting the messages you hear, stop and confront them with ones that are constructive. If you hear yourself saying," I did everything I was told and look how it ended," ask yourself if the advice you were receiving was valid and within your best interest. While the words may have been intended to be well meaning, they were coming from the perspective and life experiences of the speaker. They are often prefaced with "shoulds," "ought tos," "nevers," "always," and "musts". Think about messages such as, "You should never admit your mistakes" or "Always accept less than what you hope for." Internalizing these messages will not serve you when you need to be acting from your strengths and talents.

> *"Feeling like I was a "quitter," a failure.*
> *What am I doing trying to do this job? Can't take stress and*
> *abuse anymore. Regret for not leaving earlier."*
> – MW, Project manager

One method for challenging negative messages is to counter them with ones that are in direct opposition. If your self-talk includes statements such as, "You're such a failure," replace it with, "I'm such a success." Then list all the events in your life that support the positive statement which will become your new belief system. These can be large or small successes. Passing your driving test, graduating from high school, taking the risk of asking someone on a date, and moving into your first apartment all qualify for the list. Add to the list until you have a minimum of ten achievements. Read through them at least three times each day for the next month. You can even record and listen to them on your phone. Eventually, the messages will encode themselves in your neural pathways and become a natural way of thinking.

Exercise: List the negative messages you play in your head based on the following sentence starters:

I am ____

I should ____

I ought to ____

I never ____

I always____

I must ____

Now list the negative messages you hear from those around you:

You are ____

You should ____

You ought to ____

You never ____

You always ____

You must ____

For each of the statements above, think of incidents that challenge them or new ways that you can approach a situation. For example, "I always accept less than what I am worth" can be challenged with, "I ask for what I deserve based on the contributions I make to my company." Read each of your new messages daily and outline a plan to support them.

Affirmation:

I recognize that negative messages are often rooted in fear or past experiences, and reframe them with empowering and supportive self-talk.

Regain your feeling of control

"To be in hell is to drift; to be in heaven is to steer."
– George Bernard Shaw

During times of transition, one of the greatest needs a person has is to regain control of his or her life. Whatever has precipitated the change causes a shift in the status quo so that what was familiar is no longer present. Imagine a mobile in perfect balance until someone or something disrupts that balance. It will take time before it returns to its former state, but it will not be exactly the same in terms of its position in space. It will be in balance once more until the next disruption occurs.

> *"There was a plethora of mental thoughts with a highly rigorous process for "off boarding." Even with the support and presentations that helped, it was overwhelming. The more I saw this as a life adventure beginning, the more focused I became and I also referred to guides for remaining resilient."*
> – JB, Administrative Professional

In the process of making the transition from working in the field of education to furthering my skills and interest in becoming a career coach, I felt very much like that mobile. I had established myself through years of work and dedication to a point where I was serving on work-related committees and presenting at national conferences. Now I felt like I was starting at square one since I was the new kid on the block. My self-confidence was shaken to the core as I gathered experience in my new line of work. Even though I had been successful in my work as a career development specialist in the schools, I was now working with a very different population. I knew that it would not be an easy task to ascend to the same level where I had been when I left my previous field, but I had the experience of moving into other previously uncharted territories when I was hired into positions that had not existed before.

Sometimes when you have nothing else to base your direction upon, you realize that you can't really make many mistakes because those above you have nothing to compare it with. For me, the best way to regain a sense of control was to realize that I was growing my job in response to the needs I observed. I eventually gathered enough experience to be at the level I had been at in my prior field. It's estimated that it takes about 10,000 hours to develop a high level of competence for a specific task or role. It's not by accident that managerial positions generally require five years of work experience when one considers that the average person works about 2,000 hours per year.

One way to feel like you're in control of your life is to think small. This message seems to fly in the face of all the advice you hear from the gurus of the world who tell you to set your sights on grandiose goals. But it isn't actually contradictory to what they are saying. Small, calculated steps will be more successful than ones that are riskier and unclear. If you have been recently unemployed, start by making a list of what needs to be done today. If you qualify for unemployment benefits, have you completed the necessary paperwork to initiate payments? Have you checked your bank account balance to estimate how long it can support being out of work based on current expenses? Have you identified ways to reduce your spending to cover your basic needs? These questions are designed to deal with your immediate situation. Many individuals who are out of work will ignore doing this because they fear that their financial reality was not well planned. This is a definite contributor to feeling out of control. Make sure that you have a least a six-month reserve in place to provide for your needs during this time of transition.

"I opted in for taking an early retirement package after being at a reputable technology company for

> *25 years. At first I was in a state of shock, felt despair about the loss of a strong work family culture and [I was] apprehensive. By the last workday I shifted my sentiments to realizing that this was the time in my life to "remake myself." [Feeling] more optimistic."*
> —JB, Administrative Professional

Realize the need for rituals and incorporate them into your routine. Rituals are behaviors that assist in reducing stress, especially after a loss. I once applied for a position that was a perfect fit for my skills and experience. I anxiously awaited the call to schedule the interview that would lead to my hiring. Much to my surprise, the response came in the form of a letter thanking me for my interest, but I was not even being considered for the first round of interviews. After my initial disappointment, I took the letter to my balcony and lit a match to it. As the flames arose I envisioned the close of that chapter in my life and was determined to focus on finding something better. I felt a sense of lightness following the ritual of burning the letter. The last thing I needed to do was to keep it as a reminder of the past. If there is anyone that you believe has treated you unfairly, writing a letter to them stating your case and then burning it can unburden you of the obstacles that can keep you stuck. Some people perform rituals before they go into a job interview or make a sales call. Do you ever notice athletes who do a victory dance when they score points? This behavior appears to be universal. If it helps boost your confidence and reinforces a sense of control, then feel free to use it.

Learn to be proactive rather than reactive. Take responsibility for your part in life and take action to achieve your goals. I have worked with clients who knew well advance of their lay off that it was coming. Had they been proactive they would have been pursuing new opportunities earlier. The best time to look for a job is when they have a job. The energy that you take into your job search when you're employed is different from that when you're feeling desperate for anything that pays. When you find yourself saying, "I'll take anything that comes along," you are in reactive mode. Keep your lines of communication with your network open at all times. This is the value of social media. Maintain a list of your contacts and reach out to them on a regular basis. Something as simple as wishing them a happy birthday or anniversary will keep you connected. Be looking for ways that you can be helpful to them rather than to always be on the asking end. Be cautious of using this time to blame others for your situation. This will promote victim mentality thinking that will prevent you from moving forward. Always be mindful of the part you played and be willing to change what you can about yourself.

Exercise: On the following page, in **Column A** identify three times when you felt like the circumstances of a situation controlled you. In **Column B** write what you had expected to happen. In **Column C** write what actually occurred. In **Column D** write what you could have done to control the situation. In **Column E** write the likelihood of your actions making a difference in the situation.

Column A	Column B	Column	Column D	Column E
Situation	Expectations	C What actually occurred	What I could have done	Likelihood of it making a difference

Use this time to step back and ask yourself what it is that you really want in life. This involves reflecting on your goals and values and making decisions based on them. Do you find the work that you have been doing motivates you to continue on that path, or is there something that you have always wanted to do that you have kept on the back burner for years? Is this the time to reconsider an earlier interest and identify ways to pursue it? Think of situations in which your best shines forth. What were you doing, and is it possible to translate this into an employment opportunity? Have you been spending your life fulfilling the dreams of others such as your parents or spouse? What would you be happiest doing if you didn't have their input? What would it take to live your own dream? Would you feel more in control of your life if you chose to pursue that dream?

During times of transition, it's tempting to adopt coping mechanisms that will hamper your progress. It's more difficult to develop resilience when you're using your time in unproductive ways. Staying up late watching reruns on television, excessive drinking, and gambling will serve as distractions in the moment and prevent you from focusing on the tasks that will ultimately alter your situation. Look at the ways at which you're handling your current stress levels and commit to changing those that are problematic. You can choose to limit the distractions by placing a time limit on them. Think of them as potential rewards that will follow the completion of specific work-related tasks such as reading about current trends in your industry or making contact with someone in your network. If you find that it's difficult to adhere to time limits, you may want to take a more serious look at your behavior. Should you cross over into addictive behavior, it can add to the challenges of transition.

When unproductive or destructive behaviors begin to interfere with your progress, consider what might be the root cause, and be willing to deal with it. The onset of these behaviors may be acute (a job loss) or chronic (a deeper psychological issue). If you're aware of a pattern of these behaviors as you experience changes, consider seeking out professional support. This awareness may come from you directly or through comments made by those around you. The source is not as important as the action you take to address these behaviors.

Affirmation:

I am reclaiming my self-control during my job search by taking ownership of my thoughts, emotions, and behaviors.

Make time for fun and pleasure

"Dance as though no one is watching you;
love as though you have never been hurt before,
sing as though no one can hear you,

live as though heaven is on earth."
– Alfred Souza

Our word for playful activities is recreation. When you break the word down it becomes "re-creation." It's a re-creation of your energy, a recharging of your physical and mental systems. How do you feel after engaging in time to play? There is a sense of revitalization and renewal. If you were feeling down, your spirits are lifted. When you return to work, you may find that your ability to concentrate and problem solve has improved. Perhaps turning a work-related problem into a game or play might be a more effective solution than expending more mental energy on it.

It's in your nature to be playful and have fun. You're born with a natural curiosity of the world around you, and play provides an opportunity to stretch your mind and body. It allows your imagination to be free and explore endless possibilities. If you doubt this, take some time to observe a small child surrounded by both familiar and unfamiliar objects. If it's a one-year-old, the object is likely to be inserted into the mouth since that is one of the primary sources of sensory input. This activity will be accompanied by cooing and laughter as the child moves from one object to the next. There are no rules to follow that constrain the amount of time spent nor the uses for each object.

One activity that appears to be universal among children centers on the kitchen and the attraction for pots and pans and what can be done with them. My mother used to comment that with all the toys we had, we would still go into the kitchen cupboards, pull out several large pots and bang them with a large wooden or metal spoon. It's likely that drumming is one of our most ancient forms of self-expression. Through it we learn rhythms and patterns that are translated into other forms. Other similar activities include constructing tents from blankets stretched over couches and chairs in the living room. When it comes to imagination, it doesn't require sophisticated or elaborate equipment to entertain the mind and body. My guess is that an infant engaged in play will rarely express negative emotions while doing so unless a sense of frustration erupts when the object of his attention doesn't do what he hopes it would.

When you're feeling stress from a change in your life, make time for play. Consider choosing activities that have the fewest rules. If there are rules, feel free to suspend them. This is a time to experience freedom from adult constraints. I remember spending time with my friend's four-year-old daughter. She decided that she wanted to color in her coloring book. I suggested that we have fun and choose colors that were definite rule breakers. We decided we would color the characters' faces green, or blue, or whatever we wanted, and we didn't have to stay in the lines. Once we agreed that faces and arms didn't have to have flesh tones, the color possibilities became endless and our creativity led us to multicolored limbs.

The sources of play are endless. You can choose ones that take place in any type of environment. If you prefer being outdoors, you can swim, hike, bike, skate, or participate in team sports such as soccer, baseball, or tennis. If you're more of an indoor person, you can play board games, ping-pong, billiards, or go dancing. Some activities can be played in either setting such as swimming, basketball, ice skating, or running. There is a wide range to the amount of concentration needed for play. Walking through the park observing the beauties of nature requires much less concentration than playing a team sport in which you must be aware of the other players and rules. I have read that, for play to exert a positive effect of your physical and mental being, you should plan to spend at least 20 minutes engaging in it.

If there is an activity you have always wanted to pursue such as ballroom dancing or painting, think about signing up for an informal class offered through the community. You don't have to worry about receiving a passing grade as a measure of competence. All you have to do is to show up and have fun. Back in the 70s, I enrolled in a class to learn how to disco. Having a different partner each week taught me an appreciation for what it takes to choreograph the movements to make them look effortless. At the end of the class, you can decide whether or not it's something you would do on a regular basis.

Exercise: What activities do you engage in for fun? For each activity you list, indicate how often you do it. Is it daily, weekly, monthly, or annually? Now write if you engage in it alone or with others. Next, indicate if it's a spontaneous or planned activity. Finally, identify if it is an activity guided by rules or no rules. What does the information you gathered say about you and how you have fun in life? Are you engaging in enough fun to keep you energized and alert? If not, what changes can you make to achieve that?

Activity	Frequency	Alone/ With Others	Spontaneous/ Planned	Rules/No rules

While it may seem at the time that there is little humor to be found in your current situation, maintaining a sense of humor while going through a transition can help to alleviate stress. There are physiological effects brought on by humor, including the reduction of stress hormones. When you're engaged in humor you suspend reality. Sitting in a theater in Las Vegas listening to Rita Rudner deliver joke after joke about her view of life brought about the kind of tears that accompany uncontrollable laughter. You can imagine what my mood was like after leaving that performance. Try experiencing anger and laughter simultaneously. It's like trying to keep your eyes open when you sneeze.

You may wonder what there is to laugh about when you're out of work and not sure where your next meal is coming from. Humor is not about minimizing your current situation. It's about taking time out from the serious to see another lighter side of life. When you laugh, chemical changes occur in the brain; serotonin is released resulting in improved focus and objectivity. Humor connects you with others, reducing feelings of isolation and loneliness. It may be the social aspect of laughter that provides the greatest benefits. Imagine the effect that this has when you're in a room filled with people laughing aloud at a well-delivered joke or story. Laughter rarely occurs in isolation; it requires a sender and a receiver—even when you're alone and reading a joke or a cartoon there are still two entities at play.

Remember that there is a difference between being funny and having a sense of humor. There are individuals who seem to have a natural talent for telling a joke or funny story. Their listeners are mesmerized by the way they weave their words. If you're good at telling jokes, they can serve as a way to bond with others. Some people are better at one-liners than they are at holding an audience's attention with a complete story. Find a way of expressing humor that works best for you. What is most critical is that humor is a universal connector. Sometimes we are at our funniest when we aren't trying. You can't force humor, so just be open to expressing it. With humor, timing is everything.

Note that there may be a tendency to laugh at someone rather than with someone when you're under stress. Think before you utter words that may do more harm than good. This is less about humor and more about projecting your own feelings of inadequacy and insecurity on to others. Be willing to own what you are thinking and feeling and share it in healthy ways. One of the most memorable definitions is related to a form of humor known as sarcasm, which literally means "to tear the flesh." What is it like for you to be the brunt of such humor and how can you avoid it?

Choose to spend time with friends who are naturals when it comes to humor. Notice how you feel before you begin interacting with them and then again after being amused by their words and actions. You will find yourself to feel more motivated and engaged after a healthy bout of laughter. Identify what makes you laugh. Is it watching a favorite comedy on television or the movies? Is it playing games that produce unexpected responses? Is it spending time with pets and children who are spontaneous? Is it reading jokes or watching videos online of people engaged in funny situations? Whatever makes you laugh, be sure to incorporate time for it throughout your day.

While laughter is important, don't forget to smile. Watch what happens when you smile at the cashier in the grocery store or the receptionist at the doctor's office. It's a nonverbal way of connecting with others. A smile can initiate a conversation that can open doors. Would you prefer to talk to someone who was poker-faced or one who greeted you with a smile? Smiling makes you more approachable and likable, but only if your smile is genuine. You can usually tell if someone is flashing a forced smile at you, which can cause you to question their motives. When it's real it can leave a lasting impression. I instruct my clients to keep a mirror in front of them when they are participating in a phone interview and make frequent checks to make sure they are smiling. Smiling helps to reduce stress by releasing endorphins, and the energy that is generated by your smile can be transmitted to the listener and give you an advantage. Smiles are free, so use them frequently.

Exercise: List five ways that you invite humor into your life, i.e. reading cartoons, watching comedies, etc. Become aware of the frequency that you experience humor in each of these five areas over a one-month period by placing a checkmark in the box next to it every time it occurs. What does this information tell you about its presence in your life?

Sources of Humor	Frequency within a month
1.	
2.	
3.	
4.	
5.	

Affirmation:

I recognize that balance and enjoyment are essential for my overall well-being and success.

Connect with others

"I like to think that as I get older I'm getting better at spending time with people who have qualities that make them worth spending time with."
– Samantha Power

When you consciously choose to share your time with others, you forget your own problems for the time being. Your focus is on giving, not getting. There are so many opportunities for giving of your time and talent, especially to those who may be less fortunate than you. It always helps to put your problems in perspective when you see someone who has even less than you do. You begin to see that life is not always about what you have, but more about how you make do with what you have been given. For the time that you're giving to others, your gift is experiencing the moment.

Look for ways that you can donate your time to activities with the elderly, children, adults with special needs, and the homeless. Perhaps you have a talent for teaching a specific skill. There are those who would benefit from your ability to teach reading in a literacy program or how to repair bicycles for children. You may have an inclination to work with animals. There are many ways that you can do this. You may choose to work in a shelter assisting with the pet adoption process or providing animals with daily exercise. If you're more clinically oriented there are opportunities to help provide treatment to animals or to support the veterinarians and veterinary technicians with spaying and neutering procedures. In addition to giving to others, you will be building new skill sets that can be transferred into employment opportunities.

One positive side effect to volunteering your time is that it gives others a chance to observe you at work. While you may only consider paid employment to constitute work experience, work covers both paid and unpaid positions. When I was unemployed a number of years ago while transitioning from one field to another, I volunteered to do career coaching. The feedback to the agency from those I worked with led to me being hired on a permanent basis. When people can observe your actual job performance, you become a much more viable candidate for employment since you're demonstrating both hard and soft skills. It becomes easier to determine if you're a good fit for their culture.

> *"Volunteering [is important at this time].*
> *Helping others makes me feel good."*
> –HR, Finance Professional

Exercise: Name three people (can also include pets) you enjoy spending time with. Next to each name write what it is about them that you enjoy.

1. ____

2. ____

3. ____

Name three opportunities you have for volunteering your time. How are you involved in that experience?

1. ____

2. ____

3. ____

What groups do you belong to and participate with on a regular basis? This can include a church group, a sports team, a professional organization, a charitable organization, etc.

1. ___________________   2. ___________________

3. ___________________   4. ___________________

5. ___________________   6. ___________________

7. ___________________   8. ___________________

9. ___________________   10. ___________________

We can connect with others on both a figurative and a literal level. The largest organ in the human body is the skin. Your skin is permeated with tiny nerve endings designed to carry vital information to the brain where it's interpreted and acted upon instantaneously. It can warn us of danger, provide information on how an object feels, differentiate between hot and cold, and serve as a source of pleasure or pain. You are biologically programmed to connect with your surroundings through touch. When you're deprived of contact with other human beings it's referred to as "skin hunger." You create a bond with others when you engage in physical touch.

As an undergraduate psychology major, I read through many research studies. One particular study that left a deep impression on me was that of the wire monkey. Baby monkeys were removed from their mothers and provided a choice of two surrogate mother monkeys. One of the monkeys was constructed of wire and the other of cloth. The wire monkey could dispense food while the cloth monkey did not. The researcher learned that the baby monkeys chose the warmth of the cloth monkey over the food offered by the wire monkey. This demonstrated that the need for warmth and affection was even stronger than the need for food. We find this to also be true in infants who were provided limited physical touch when they were born. They did not thrive at the same rate as infants who were held.

Human touch is one of the earliest forms of communication. Bonds of trust and affection are forged within the first year of life. Notice mothers with their newborn babies and how much time is spent engaged in holding. If you have any questions about the significance of human touch, seek out its presence in the world of art. There are countless portraits of mothers cradling their children and lovers embracing. I recall, as a child, the many times that I bumped my head or pinched my fingers in a door or drawer. My mother's favorite expression was, "Let me kiss it and make it better." In a matter of seconds, the pain subsided and I was running off on my next adventure. It was as if a mother's kiss was a miracle cure. Most likely it was the result of the release of chemicals, including oxytocin, that create a sense of well-being. Oxytocin helps to reduce blood pressure and stress as well as enhance your mood. Even a gesture as simple as holding someone's hand can produce a calming response.

When you're going through a transition, look for sources of genuine hugs. The need for physical contact does not decrease over time. In other words, we do not outgrow our need for hugs. It's said that as humans we need a minimum of four hugs a day for survival and at least 12 hugs a day for growth. Hugs can be delivered in a variety of ways, depending on the strength of the relationship. There is the full hug which involves the two individuals having their entire bodies in contact with one another. Then there is the half-hug in which you stand next to the person using one arm to hug them as they hug you in return. Finally, there is the A-frame hug in which two people lean into one another making minimal body contact. I find it important to identify people with whom I can share a full hug to have the most benefit.

Have you ever had a friend rub your shoulders or give you a back rub? When they do, somehow all the tension you have been storing seems to flow out of your body. As part of the warm-ups we have in a large chorus to which I belonged, the conductor had us line up and do back and shoulder rubs. It seemed to be one of the favorite parts of rehearsal. This is especially true when you consider that most of us have been working all day and are carrying that stress with us. It also releases oxytocin which contributes to the bonding between us to create a unified sound. If you can't afford to use the services of a massage therapist, think about someone you know and trust who would be willing to give you a back rub. Offer to do the same for others. It's important to be discerning in who you enlist for this activity. Knowing the other person and feeling comfortable exchanging physical contact is a key element.

Exercise:

How do you prefer to give and receive human contact?

____

____

____

____

____

Monitor your human contact during the week by marking its frequency below each day listed.

Sunday	Monday	Tuesday	Wednesday	Thursday	Friday	Saturday

Where are you in meeting your quota for daily human contact?

0 - 3 = Deprived   4 - 7 = Survival   8 - 11 = Maintenance   12 = Growth

What do you need to do to increase human contact to achieve the Growth state?

____

____

____

Affirmation:

I trust in the power of connection and the potential it holds for my career knowing that building meaningful relationships and networks can open doors to new opportunities.

Look for positive meaning in your life

*"To think what is true, to sense what is beautiful
and to want what is good, hereby the spirit
finds purpose of a life in reason."*
– Johann Gottfried Herder

When you're feeling the pressures associated with transition, there can be a tendency to question your very being. Thoughts such as, "Maybe it would have been better if I had never been born" or "Does my being here even matter?" may enter your mind, but are best left not entertained. You may remember the character of George Bailey in Frank Capra's 1946 film, *It's a Wonderful Life*. It's Christmas and George is down on his luck and is contemplating suicide, believing that his presence on earth has been useless. It isn't until his guardian angel, Clarence, intervenes to point out what life without George in it would have meant for his loved ones and his community. In the end, George learns what his purpose is and embraces life with new enthusiasm and hope. We can all identify with George at some level which contributed to this being one of the most memorable and enduring films made. Resilience gives you reason to survive despite difficult or traumatic events.

We are constantly seeking answers to what our purpose for being here is to begin with. Are we simply here to live out a period of days before slipping into nonexistence? Do we arrive with a predetermined plan for filling out a karmic contract? Is there a mission that each of us has been programmed to follow with our goal being to discover what that mission is? There is no definitive answer to this. Each of you will need to figure that out for yourself. **What does matter is that *you matter*.** It's only when you accept this to be true that you will make the most of your life.

Begin each day by asking, "What can I do to make a positive difference in my life and the lives of those around me today?" How can you use your gifts and talents in a way that makes life better? Keep track of the times that you do this. Remember the key is to have a positive effect. Can you do this by taking time to listen to someone who is having problems, doing the best you can on the task that is in front of you, or helping someone carry their groceries? In terms of yourself, did you take time to get the proper rest, eat properly, and exercise today? All of this is evidence that you believe that you matter. One way to connect with people during the day is to read the name badge of the person who is providing a service and address them by name. It may only to thank them or it may lead to a full conversation, depending on the time available. I have lost count of the number of flight attendants who have told me that I made their day in the short time we were together. Think of what it's like when you're constantly interacting with the public during the day and yet are treated as if you are invisible. It doesn't take much effort to be positive.

At the end of the day take inventory of what you have done for yourself and others and savor the feelings that accompany that. If you have experiences that brought up negative thoughts and feelings, think about what you can do to alter those in the future. Perhaps you were impatient with someone on the telephone or were annoyed with the heavy traffic when you wanted to be home early. What can you do differently should those same situations occur tomorrow? When you receive a call from a telemarketer you can choose to be courteous, reminding yourself that this is how they make a living. When in traffic use the time to observe your surroundings and muse over what the day was like for other drivers. This is a world in which we are all traveling on a journey together. Your overall purpose in life today is to make it as pleasant a journey by being of service whenever possible.

At the same time that you're seeking to find your purpose for your life as a whole, ask yourself what your purpose is in the work you do. If my overall purpose is to be of service to others, this can be carried out in the work I do as a career coach. Your purpose may be as a healer, a teacher, a builder, a planner, or an artist. Your purpose can play itself out in various occupations, and this can be helpful information when you're in transition. Could this be the time for you to consider expressing your purpose in a different fashion? If you're a teacher, you might think about doing this in a different setting with a different population. Perhaps you were a high school Spanish teacher and now you would like to work with adults from Spanish speaking countries who are wanting to learn English. There are a number of options available to you in carrying out your purpose which will give positive meaning to your life.

Seek out a work environment that feeds that meaning and aligns with your purpose and values. You will have a greater satisfaction in the work you do. If you find yourself in a setting that conflicts with who you are, ask yourself if the price you're paying to remain there is worth it. Be willing to leave it if the price you're paying is too great. I have had clients come to me at such a crossroads in their worklife, and we began to create a plan for them to exit with dignity and integrity. For some, the decision to end their job led to a new beginning. For others simply having the intention to leave coincided with unexpected changes at work such as a difficult manager being transferred to a different department. I have had to make that difficult choice in the past myself, and it wasn't easy. Once I made that decision, I could search for new opportunities that made each day more fulfilling. Remember that nothing in life is permanent. What exists today will eventually change. Resilience will play a critical part in helping you step into your new role.

Exercise: For each day in the next month write five positive actions that you have taken to make a difference in the lives of others. When you have completed the exercise, look for themes and patterns. How can you take this information into the work you do?

Date	Actions

Date	Actions

Date	Actions

Date	Actions

What themes and patterns do you notice based on your actions?

Affirmation:

I choose to find the positive meaning in my life during my job search, acknowledging the strengths, talents, and achievements that have brought me to this point.

Be mindful of words of encouragement

*"Treat people as if they were what they ought to be and
you help them to become what they are capable of being."*
– Johann Wolfgang von Goethe

During my first year in college, I was enrolled in the required freshman English class. Following our first writing assignment, my instructor chose to project my paper onto the screen with a large red F on it. She then proceeded to announce how this was the way NOT to write a paper. Needless to say, I was mortified. It wasn't until years later when I was working on my doctorate, that another instructor had a profound effect on my writing skills. The assignment was to write a paper on a specific medical condition. I chose the topic of asthma and integrated research with information gathered from three friends who had grown up with this condition. When the instructor returned my paper the pages were covered in green remarks. My first thoughts returned me to that earlier English class, and I dreaded reading the comments that he had written. But this time there were no negatives. One comment after another referred to the content and the approach that I had taken. At the end of the paper, he suggested that I submit it for publication. This was a far cry from my earlier experience and motivated me to continue to develop and improve my writing skills. Encouragement matters.

During times of transition, you enter a place filled with uncertainty and upheaval. The world that held familiarity and security has been transformed and often lacks a definitive end. It's at this time that you need to hear words of encouragement and not judgment or condemnation. What awaits you on the other side of transition can be very unlike what preceded it. You may have been married for thirty years in what you thought was a stable relationship and suddenly have your spouse inform you that she wants a divorce. You learn that the money you invested to support you in retirement is a fraction of what you had planned for due to a drastic drop in the stock market. You work for a company for twenty-five years and are told that on Monday you will no longer be employed there. This is not the time to listen to people tell you about what you should have done to avoid this. This is the time to garner moral support so that you can have the courage to take the next steps.

What words of encouragement would you want to hear most? When you're initially confronted with news that something significant is about to change in your life, how helpful is it to hear, "Don't worry. It'll get better before you know it" or "It could be worse." While these statements may be well intentioned, they don't offer much in the way of hope or empathy. It would be helpful to hear someone say to you, "This has got to be tough to deal with. I don't know what to say right now that would make this any easier. Just know that I am here to help in any way I can." Or, "I am just a phone call away if you need to talk." While working on my counseling degree, the one phrase we were taught never to say to anyone going through a painful experience was, "I know just how you feel." Even if you have suffered a similar type of loss, no two people work through it in exactly the same way. You want the other person to be respectful of the circumstances surrounding the change and allow you the needed time to process it.

The event that precipitated the change will distance itself as time passes, but that doesn't mean that the emotional impact will necessarily lessen. Your friends may be there for you initially, and that is critical for getting through the first days of transition. In the case of having your employment terminated, the transition to your next position could last for weeks, months, or even years. This is when on-going encouragement from your support group matters most. Let people know what you need most at this time. On the days you feel discouraged, ask people you trust to describe one or more traits that they admire in you. Write their comments on post-its and display them in prominent places in your home to remind you of your worth.

Keep a log of the actions you have taken to change your situation. This information is useful on the days when you feel like you're afloat on a sea with no land in sight. As you read through the actions you have taken in the past, think of ones that will be helpful today. Remind yourself that, if you did them before, you can do them again today. Ask yourself what the outcome of the action was and if there is anything that you can do differently to improve your chances for success. This might include adding the name of a contact who could introduce you to a new opportunity.

At the same time that you're benefitting from encouraging words from others, don't forget to offer the same in kind. Remember the words from a familiar song that, "I get by with a little help from my friends." In positively sharing with others you bolster your own sense of self-esteem.

When you see someone else who is struggling, reach out with support. Remind them that they don't need to go through this transition alone. Loneliness and isolation are challenging to someone who is dealing with loss and uncertainty. Let people know how much you appreciate their presence in your life and be sure to maintain those lifelines. There are so many vehicles for encouraging people. You can send a card, an email, a text message, or make a phone call. Just connecting with others can alter your mood and get you over the rough spots.

Exercise: In the space below make a list of the actions you have taken to move toward achieving your goal. Give yourself credit for it no matter how large or small. Next to it write your words of encouragement in the form of positive self-talk. For example, the action may be **I scheduled a meeting with John to brainstorm ideas for job options.** Your words of encouragement would be **I am proud of myself for making that call.** When looking for words of encouragement, focus on the positive feelings that would accompany them such as happy, glad, hopeful, excited.

Actions Taken	Words of Encouragement

Affirmation:

I choose to embrace and amplify the positive impact words of encouragement that affirm that I have what it takes to succeed in my job search.

Have a practical plan for the day

"Apathy can be overcome by enthusiasm, and enthusiasm can only be aroused by two things: first, an idea, with takes the imagination by storm, and second, a definite intelligible plan for carrying that ideal into practice."
– Arnold J. Toynbee

One benefit to being employed is that you have a structured routine for your day. You're typically expected to start and end work at specific times associated with carrying out your job duties. Even if you own your own business, there are tasks that must be performed for you to sustain yourself.

"Setting a consistent wake-up time. Set[ting] up a home office. Creating an actionable to-do list."
-TH, Program Manager

All of this contributes to predictability making life less stressful.

When your work situation changes, your routine is disrupted. The alarm doesn't ring at 6:00 AM and there is no urgency in starting the day. Eventually, the lack of routine becomes your routine. This contributes to a sense of apathy resulting from the disconnection from the work setting that provides for many of your social and emotional needs. You may find that you have lost interest in activities that you previously found to be stimulating. You substitute endless hours of watching television or surfing the net for performing meaningful tasks. Days become weeks without accomplishing much. You isolate yourself from friends and family because it's too much effort to spend time with them.

This is the time when it's most important to create a plan for how you will spend your waking hours. You may find it advantageous to write out your plan in 15-minute segments. If you have worked in a job that required you to be up at 6:00 AM, you may either continue with that schedule or allow yourself an extra hour to sleep. Once you have established the time to begin your day, add specific activities to fill it. This includes taking time to eat a nutritional breakfast, shower, and dress for the day. Where would you insert time for exercise? What time would you allot for your job search? Some people believe that sitting at the computer completing online applications is all that is necessary when conducting a job search. Then they wonder why no interviews are forthcoming.

Make sure that you're going to bed early enough so that you're waking rested and ready for the next day's tasks. Sleep is your body's vehicle for maintaining and repairing itself. It's hard to concentrate when you're only functioning on a few hours' sleep. If you enjoy watching television before retiring, plan to watch a program that will leave you feeling relaxed, not stressed. Ending your day by watching the nightly news may not be within your best interest if you're viewing scenes of crime and violence. Those are the last images you take into your consciousness and could affect your ability to fall asleep quickly as well as the dreams you might have. If you plan to be awake by 7:00 AM, look to having lights out by 11:00 PM. Some people benefit by listening to meditation tapes or soft music to end their day.

Give yourself less structured time during the weekend. Perhaps you can enjoy a more leisurely breakfast before heading out for some fun activities with friends or getting to those household chores you have been putting off over the last few months. Whatever you choose to do, make a mental note of how you felt as you were doing it. Did you feel satisfied when you cleaned out your closet or the garage? Were you exhilarated after a three-hour hike? Did you lose track of time reading your favorite book?

Exercise: Using your phone, a day planner, or a self-designed calendar, create a schedule for your day. Look at building in 15-minute increments that will give you more flexibility. You may choose to carve out a specific time to wake up, schedule your first activity after breakfast, and proceed from there until 4:00 or 5:00 PM. Build in exercise and recreation to balance out your day.

Affirmation:

I start each day with clarity and intention, setting clear goals and outlining the specific tasks I need to accomplish to ensure that I allocate my time and energy effectively.

Key Learning Points

- It's important to meet physical, emotional, and social needs during transition.
- Engaging in positive self-talk can affect outcomes.
- Taking time for recreational activities and laughter serves to energize the mind and body.
- Maintaining a structured day supports a focus for carrying out needed tasks.
- Identifying strengths and abilities serves to differentiate oneself while marketing in the workplace.
- Being proactive rather than reactive is useful in establishing a sense of self-control.
- An individual's purpose in life serves as a guidance system when making decisions on which steps to take.

What is your story around resilience as you read through this chapter? What was it that triggered your thoughts around this?

CHAPTER SIX

Commitment

"Unless commitment is made, there are only promises and hopes... but no plans."
– Peter Drucker

Commitment self-assessment quiz

Mark **Yes** or **No** as it applies to your life today.

1. I would describe myself as a person who can be counted on to complete a task.	Yes	No
2. I have a list of people in my network who I can contact for support.	Yes	No
3. I schedule the time I need to meet deadlines.	Yes	No
4. I follow up with others in a timely manner.	Yes	No
5. I am willing to postpone an activity that would prevent me from meeting a deadline.	Yes	No
6. I am aware of what contributes to my procrastination and can address it when it occurs.	Yes	No
7. I reward myself intermittently while working on a project rather than waiting until it is completed.	Yes	No
8. I am clear on what I want to accomplish and what success will look like.	Yes	No
9. I know how to create a strategic plan for achieving my goals.	Yes	No
10. I am generally confident in my ability to achieve my goals.	Yes	No

To determine your score, count the number of **Yes** statements. ____

8-10 You indicate a **high** degree of ability within this area.

4-7 You indicate a **moderate** degree of ability within this area.

1-3 You indicate a **low** degree of ability within this area.

Commitment defined

Commitment involves the act of binding yourself to a course of action on an intellectual or emotional level. You're more likely to carry out your commitment when you share it with others. Think about a habit that you wanted to change. Perhaps it had to do with dropping 20 pounds or no longer smoking. You will spend a considerable amount of time mulling over the decision before you decide to share it with someone else. Once you do you are more likely to be successful with achieving it. But your desire needs to be paired with a specific plan for how you will make this happen. For example, to drop 20 pounds you will need to consciously adopt a different lifestyle by including regular exercise, altering your eating habits, and getting more rest. If you're a person who is driven by internal motivation, you can accomplish this by monitoring your activities on a daily basis. If you need external motivation, find an accountability partner with whom you can share your progress. Since you know yourself better than anyone else, identify ways that you typically sabotage your improvement plans, and identify ways to counter that.

The years that I took to complete my doctorate were largely due to my highly creative efforts to avoid focusing on it. I paid a dissertation coach to help me through the process. I tracked the days that I actively worked on writing with the promise that I would pay a penalty for each day that nothing was done. Days stretched into weeks with nothing to show for the time. It didn't seem to matter to me that I was spending money on a task that obviously held little value to me. It wasn't until my major advisor informed me that I had two semesters to complete my program or I would be out with no degree to show for it that I found the motivation to complete my dissertation. That earned my complete attention, and I did whatever it took to finish on schedule. The moral of the story is to set a deadline with a set of consequences strong enough to keep you on task and stick to a plan for achieving it.

If you're seeking employment, promise yourself that you are absolutely committed to your job search and that you will do everything in your power to find work that fits who you are and what you have to offer. Begin by clarifying what it is that you want to do and where you want to do it. I have clients create a list of tasks they would be performing, what the work environment would be like, who their coworkers and customers would be in terms of positive behaviors, and what their benefits would include. When opportunities present themselves, they can match them to their lists. They become committed to working toward the best fit. It may mean taking an interim position to cover living expenses, but their ultimate goal is to continue to find the job that best utilizes their skills and experience.

Tap into your network

"There is no shame in asking for help;
it is one the most courageous things you'll ever do and will
lead to greater connection with those around you."
– Laura Lane

We live in a society that defines success through the work that we do. Being unemployed, especially over a period of time, carries a stigma. It's as if you possess an irreparable flaw that prevents you from being hired. The truth is that what you're observing is most likely the other person projecting their fear of being out of work on to you. While many people gain a sense of identity from the work they do, that identity can be challenged at any moment in today's job market. There are no guarantees of job security and so it's always incumbent to maintain your connections before a change occurs.

It's much easier to elicit help from others when you're sure of what it is that they can do for you. Commit to the time needed to clarify your short and long-term goals. A client once told me that his strength was in communication. The first question was, "Where are they hiring people who have communication skills?" This was immediately followed up with, "Tell me where I should go to apply for that job today." You can imagine his disappointment when I responded that communication skills are used across many settings and that he needed to be more specific in what would be involved in a desired position. He would not engage in any discussion of what that position might be. Had he made a commitment to explore occupations that utilize communication as a primary task, he could have found openings that capitalized on that skill. Imagine how you might respond to someone you know who asks you to help him find work with only vague information to go by. Most people are eager to help if they know what you specifically need.

> *"Stay connected with my strong network of professionals who believe in me and advocate for my deserving to be in a better place."*
> –GW

Once you're clear in the type of work you're seeking, commit to connecting with a specific number of people who can be helpful in achieving your work-related goals. These contacts could be related to a hire or developing a specific skill. Write the names of at least 25 people you know. They can be family, friends, former classmates, co-workers, or service providers such as your barber, your mechanic, or your gardener. Next to each name list their occupation and then the company or industry they represent. Finally, write their contact information, including a recent phone number and/or email address. This list will constitute the foundation of your network. Ask yourself when the last time you had contact with this individual and what you can do to reconnect if it has been a while since that happened last.

Exercise: Commit to building your list of contacts using the form below. You will need to update it on a regular basis. This will ensure that you're staying in touch with the people on your list.

Name	Occupation	Company/ Industry	Contact Information

Name	Occupation	Company/ Industry	Contact Information

So many people express regret that they didn't keep in touch with former classmates, friends, and coworkers. They waited until they were out of work to reach out and were concerned that their efforts would be interpreted as needy and desperate. This might have been avoided had they stayed in touch which would have kept them connected. In today's world of social media, it isn't difficult to communicate with those from our past. It actually makes the initial act of reconnecting quite simple. This was the case when I was approaching my fifty-year high school reunion. Classmates whom I hadn't spoken to since we graduated were sending me requests to connect with them and I was doing the same. No one questioned why I had waited so long to do this. They were pleased that we were now communicating what had happened over the years since we graduated. Don't use the time that has passed as an excuse not to reconnect with others.

Once you have established a foundation of people you know from the past and the present, it's time to add the names of those you meet next through daily activities. If you find it valuable to join a group that is representative of your occupation, this can be a rich supply of names for your list. When I attend an event sponsored by the Chamber of Commerce or other career coaches, I make a commitment beforehand to initiate a conversation with three people I have never spoken to before and reestablish contact with two people I already know. That intention keeps me aware of my activity level and prevents me from seeking the safety of limiting my time to only one individual. Using this technique I have built quite a professional arsenal of people I can call upon when my clients are ready to conduct informational interviews. At the same time, I am making mental note of individuals I know who can benefit from the specific services of my contacts. You want this to be a reciprocal as opposed to a one-sided relationship. I might not see someone I know for several months which can warrant a quick email or telephone call to see how they are doing. Staying connected requires a conscious effort on your part and is well worth it.

Affirmation:

I embrace the power of tapping into my network, fostering a genuine sense of connection, trust, and mutual support.

Develop discipline

*"We all have dreams. But in order to make
dreams come into reality, it takes an awful lot of
determination, dedication, self-discipline, and effort."*
– Jesse Owens

Discipline consists of the ability to control your actions for the purpose of achieving your goals. It requires that you maintain your focus in spite of obstacles and distractions. We often associate discipline with athletic achievements since this is where you see the most obvious results. An athlete adopts a strict regimen that includes awakening each morning to practice specific skills, maintaining a strict diet, and getting enough sleep to repair and strengthen muscle. A commitment to a goal demands dedication and sacrifice. The desire to succeed must exceed the temptation to quit. When the impulse to settle for less emerges, the individual with self-discipline will exercise a rational approach for pushing through that conflict.

Who do you know who exemplifies self-discipline? What behaviors do they demonstrate that reflect that trait? While not everyone is blessed with a natural talent for an operatic voice or inspiring others to follow them, every one of us can learn strategies for self-discipline. This can apply to anything from shedding unwanted weight to running a marathon to writing a novel.

One such strategy is to maintain a written record of the work you do each day to achieve your goal. Once I made the decision to author a book on transition, I had to come up with a way to ensure that I would not fall victim to other activities that would distract me. Writing this book required that I be disciplined to adhere to my commitment to write 500 to 600 words each day. To achieve this I kept a daily written log that included my total word count as my starting point, the number of words at the end of my writing session, and the difference which had to meet my 500 to 600-word count. When I began to lose my motivation and interest during the actual writing, I would take out my calculator and determine how many more words were needed to meet my daily goal. It was what I needed to propel me over the finish line for that day. I eventually saw a thousand words grow to over seventy thousand. Imagine the sense of accomplishment seeing those hard numbers before me.

Exercise: For each of the goals you have developed, complete the following statement:

Today I commit to achieving my goal of ________________________

____

____

____

I will take the following actions to show my commitment to my goal:

____

____

____

____

Should I be tempted to neglect any of these actions, I will contact my accountability partner to reinforce my commitment to them and to myself.

Do something every day to work toward your goals. Sometimes the hows show up in ways that you would least expect. My clients never cease to amaze me with their stories of serendipitous events during their job searches. They may have a chance encounter with a former co-worker or a customer who shares that they know of someone who is looking for an employee with the experience and skills that the client possesses. Of course, the client has to complete the necessary documents to qualify for the interview, but the process flows easily because of the increased probability that they will be considered for the position. It isn't unheard of that once a job opportunity presents itself, it's followed by multiple opportunities. Then it becomes a matter of choosing the one that best meets their current needs and their work preferences.

What distinguishes these clients in their success is the discipline with which they conduct their job searches. They often exceed the expectations for the job search tasks assigned to them. They report how quickly they set up informational interviews, did labor market research, or sent follow-up letters after interviews, and what they learned from these actions.

Procrastination is the nemesis of most job seekers. It's often fueled by a fear or lack of information. Perhaps they are afraid to apply for a job because they have been unemployed for a significant amount of time and fear that the hiring manager won't even consider them because of it. Or they lack one of the required qualifications. Or they don't know how to fill in the blank that asks for their desired salary.

> *"Focus on the outcome and work my way back. Focus on networking. Step out of my comfort zone and then repeat the process over and over until [the] desired result [is] achieved."*
> – RP

It can be helpful to talk through your fears and insecurities to where you have a strategy for working through it. One client, who shared what they perceived as an inadequacy and faced it, went on to be hired. Procrastination is like having the rear wheels of your car stuck in mud. Pressing on the gas pedal doesn't get you any further ahead. You have to take a different action to provide some form of traction to move forward. Otherwise, all you're doing is wasting time and gas. Root out the source of the fear that stimulates procrastination and create a plan for moving through it with a firm commitment to achieve your goal. Work with an accountability partner or create a tracking system to ensure that it will happen.

Along the way make sure you're acknowledging the effort you're exerting. Reward yourself with breaks and allow for unplanned deviations. Think of a time when you were focused on achieving a goal. You were disciplined in your approach and you fully expected to have it materialize. At some unforeseen point, a new option presented itself and you decided to explore it. I recall applying for a summer job that I had been hired for the previous year. The interview was simply a formality, and I was offered the position soon afterward. In the meantime, I received a brochure outlining a new educational program that was scheduled out of state. It had always been my dream to attend such a program, so I completed the application and submitted it with no real expectation of being accepted. I was pleasantly surprised when the call came in informing me that I was invited to attend.

Now I needed to decide what to do about the position, which was a certainty and provided an income while the educational program did not. I weighed the advantages and disadvantages of each choice and subsequently sent my regrets to the agency that had hired me and planned to attend the summer training program. While there I learned how much I enjoyed the subject matter and shared what I knew with my classmates. Their feedback to the organizer was that I should be hired as a staff person for the next five summers. During those five years, I built the foundation for my current coaching practice and the premise for my dissertation. The location of the training program became the site of my future employment a number of years later. I wonder what my life would be like today if I had passed over that unexpected opportunity.

Affirmation:

I am committed to developing discipline during my job search, holding myself accountable for my actions and choices and taking responsibility for my progress and growth.

Achieve clarity

"Clarity is the most important thing. I can compare clarity to pruning in gardening. You know, you need to be clear. If you are not clear, nothing is going to happen. You have to be clear. Then you have to be confident about your vision. And after that, you just have to put a lot of work in."
– Diane von Furstenberg

To engage in commitment you need to be clear on what the object of that commitment is. You may tell others that you're committed to finding employment, but what exactly does employment include? There are often millions of jobs available at any given time. Are you committed to being hired in anything that provides financial compensation, a position with a big-name corporation, or an opportunity to learn a new trade? Lack of clarity is common among many job seekers. It may be the result of unresolved issues related to their reasons for leaving their last position, not having a sense of direction, or fear of what might happen if they finally chose to pursue a dream. Consequently, they remain stuck and confused for long periods of time.

Begin by asking yourself how clear you are when it comes to your job search. Do you have a vision of an outcome that will determine your success in finding your next position? Do you see yourself working in a busy office where co-workers are freely exchanging ideas and supporting one another to achieve their goals? Are you sitting in an airport reviewing your presentation notes as you jet off to meet with potential clients to pitch a new product that will grow their business? Are you leading a discussion on the factors that contributed to the French Revolution in a high school world history class? Set aside at least 15 minutes to engage in creating a vision for what you're doing. Clarity does not come from outside sources; it comes from within. It requires that you tap into that part of you that fuels your passion and purpose. If you find that you have a divided interest in the work you see yourself doing, you might want to explore a portfolio career that allows you to apply your skills and interests in more than one setting. For example, in seeking clarity you might work part time as a photographer and part time as a paralegal.

> *"I had ruminating thoughts such as "Where do I go from here?" "How am I going to survive?" "How am I going to provide for myself and my family?" How do I start looking for new work?"*
> – HJ, Teaching professional

Exercise: What two words or phrases best describe you? Are you inventive, entertaining, precise? Are you a negotiator, a communicator, or an educator? How do people you know see you?

1. ____

2. ____

For each word or phrase, provide three specific examples of how you have been successful with this in life.

Phrase 1: _______________________________

1. _______________________________

____

____

____

2. _______________________________

____

____

____

3. _______________________________

____

____

____

Phrase 1:

Phrase 2: ____

1. ____

____

____

____

2. ____

____

____

____

3. ____

____

____

Now list those who would benefit from these two traits. It could be an organization, an individual, or a group. Begin with those who share similar backgrounds and experiences with you. Next to each response list what the outcomes could be for that particular individual or group based on what you have to offer. Be as specific as possible.

1. ____

____

____

____

____

2. ____

____

____

____

____

____

3. ____

____

____

____

____

4. ____

____

____

____

5. ____

6. ____

7. ____

8. ____

Next, write the name(s) of individuals who you might contact to discuss each of these options beginning with #1. Make a commitment to contact them in the next three days to set up appointments to meet. Use the information they share with you to further clarify the direction you can take.

When you're seeking clarity you will need to avoid distractions. You may need to identify a location where you will not be interrupted by phone calls or emails. The quieter your environment is, the more you will stay focused on what is important to you. Unless you're working with a professional or a friend who also possesses a strong sense of clarity, attempting to identify your destination with others present will only add to uncertainty since each of the participants will have his or her own vision of where you need to go. You will leave feeling even more confused than when you started. Remember that the answers are ultimately within you.

One technique for clarifying is to create a vision board. If you're uncertain as to what your focus is, use a heading like, "My Future Life" or "What I Would Love to Do." Then gather as many magazines as you can and begin to browse through them. When you see a word or image that captures your attention, cut it out. Don't spend time analyzing why you chose that particular image. Trust that your choices come from that part of your brain that intuitively knows the direction you need to take. When you think that you have enough pieces of information, begin to arrange them on a poster board looking for patterns. Once you have arranged the images, ask yourself what the patterns are telling you about the life ahead of you. What images and words are associated with work, health, leisure, or finances? These will tell you what is most important to you today.

Now focus particularly on the messages related to work. If you have images of people, what are they doing? If you have images of objects, is there a theme to them? For example, is there a theme of technology, communication, medicine, or building? What is it about these images that call to you? What comes up for you emotionally when you focus on them? Write down whatever comes to you in the process as a way to establish clarity. What you learn can be used as the basis for the strategic plan that will be described in the next section.

Affirmation:

I know that clarity is the compass that guides me towards the right path, knowing that clarity comes from a combination of self-reflection, exploration, and taking purposeful action.

Engage in strategic planning

"Most of us fear change. Even when our minds
say change is normal, our stomachs quiver at the prospect.
But for strategists and managers today,
there is no choice but to change."
– Robert Waterman, Jr.

Imagine that you're ready for your dream vacation and plan to arrive at your destination in the next six months. Perhaps it's to visit an exotic location such as Tahiti. You're completely motivated to spend two weeks basking in the sun and enjoying all the sights that Tahiti has to offer. You have always envisioned yourself taking a walking tour of Old Papeete and picnicking on a black-sand beach at the Harrison Smith Botanical Gardens.

You notify your employer of the dates that you will be away and there is little adjustment that can be made once you do that. One month passes and you have taken no action. You haven't booked your flight, made hotel reservations, or contacted any of the companies that provide tourist information. One month after another passes and still no action is taken. Before you know it the six months have slipped by and you're days away from your scheduled vacation. You frantically begin to search the internet for flights and hotels, but everything is booked. You end up spending your two weeks in your back yard and watching reruns of 20-year-old westerns. While this is an extreme case of lack of planning, it points out what happens to your dreams when you sit idly by and wait to see where life takes you.

Strategic planning is the process of identifying the direction you're taking to reach your destination and making decisions that will increase your chances of reaching it. It involves setting goals, determining what actions are needed to achieve them, and listing the necessary resources along the way. If your plan is to vacation in Tahiti six months from now, that would be your goal. The actions needed would be to research airlines that fly there and book the one that offers the best price or departure and arrival times. You would repeat this action for making hotel reservations. You would need to check on the climate at the time of the year you plan to visit and pack suitable attire. You would need to determine if Tahiti requires a visa in addition to a passport and acquire a passport if you don't already have one. Next, you would list the resources needed. This could include contact information for travel agents and hotels. You might also want to have the name of the concierge at your hotel to make reservations for those not-to-be-missed sights. The more actions you identify, the more likely you are to experience that dream vacation. When the day of your scheduled vacation appears, you're all ready to live out that dream.

The same strategy holds true for your job search. Your next position is your destination and you will need to make specific decisions to reach it. These decisions will be based on the information that you gather along the way. The information you seek is based on the clarity you have related to your goal. It will either expedite your progress or cause you to stop and take time to consider your next steps.

While we tend to think of strategic planning as it relates to the business world, it can also be applied to your own career. Begin with where you are today. You can do this in a number of ways. What does your current resume say about you since it serves as a summary of your employment history? Does it reflect the new direction you wish to take or will its reader see it as a validation for what feels like being in a rut to you? Now is the time to pause and take stock of what you see as the next chapter in your life. What strengths, values, interests, and skills describe what you bring to the table? How do they correspond to the positions that capture your attention? How much time do you have remaining in your work life to obtain additional training and education? This information constitutes your starting point.

Next, determine what it is that you want to achieve. Describe where you want to be in one month, in six months, in one year, and in five years. You can work forward or backward in time to do this. If you're unsure of what your life will be like in each of these time periods, ask yourself what is holding you back from doing so. Are you afraid of what it will take to achieve your goals? Do you doubt your abilities? Do you lack support for your vision of your future? You will benefit from an honest appraisal of what these obstacles might be and be willing to confront them as valid or invalid. Be sure to include all areas of your life and not just the work that you do. Consider your living arrangements, your health, your finances, your relationships, and your recreational interests and how they contribute to your overall lifestyle. Again, begin from where you are and where you see yourself in the future. Remember that you're not a compartmentalized, but rather an integrated, human being. Each area of your life impacts the other areas and needs to be taken into consideration. Have fun doing this knowing that it's not etched in stone and is for your information only.

Now begin to develop a concrete plan for obtaining what you want to achieve. In the previous step you focused on the global; now focus on the specific. Look at your desired goals and be sure that they are written clearly enough so that you know when you have achieved them. Your employment goal may be to work as a systems analyst within a large company in Silicon Valley one year from now. Take time to review job postings for systems analyst positions based on what you learned in the first step of your strategic planning and evaluate your fit. If there are any gaps in your skills or experience, plan to address them through training or other learning opportunities. Ascertain whether it's realistic to have these in place within a year's time. Research the potential company as much as you can to ensure that its culture is compatible with how you function. Incorporate what you learn into your plan. Some people like to display their findings in a written list while others prefer creating schematics. Find what works for you and keep it as a work in progress.

Next, identify ways that you will be holding yourself accountable. Remember that this is about you taking 100% responsibility for your life. If you're the type of person who likes to work from charts, then you can include the tasks, resources, and deadlines for accomplishing each of them. When I ran into a writing block during the writing of my dissertation, I created a mind map with my outcome (finishing my dissertation) in the center and spokes radiating out from it with the various steps needed to accomplish that (a spoke for each chapter). From these spokes came more sub-steps to support the ones connected to them, including any outside resources I would need. Whenever I felt stuck I would refer to my mind map and choose a task to focus on. I then had the freedom to work on whatever item I felt motivated to tackle. As I completed each task I would write the word DONE next to it in red. Soon the mind map was covered in red DONES, and I was tackling those that remained. The end result was a completed dissertation.

If your resources involve specific people, develop a plan for keeping in touch with them to see where they are in following through on their commitments. You cannot afford to excuse your progress by saying to yourself that "Joe never returned my phone call," or "I'll give Anita an extension on what she said she would do because she is probably too busy to get to it." When you enlist the support of someone, build accountability into the relationship at the very beginning. Identify how you will stay in touch to ensure that they are completing their part of the agreement. You can always negotiate changes based on what you learn from them. It also confirms to them how committed you are to achieving your goals. You can also program reminders into your phone or computer that serve to prompt an action.

Finally, schedule specific times for reviewing your progress and make the necessary adjustments with the end in mind. Just as companies identify benchmarks to signal their progress toward reaching a final goal, it's important for you to segment your goal to schedule specific times to evaluate how you're doing. Start by focusing on the progress you have made, no matter how small, and give yourself credit for the effort you have taken to get this far. If you have made little progress, ask yourself what factors contributed to that. Have you taken on more than was possible for the time allotted? Is it necessary to break the tasks into smaller achievable steps? Do you question your ability to reach your goal? Are you still unclear about what your ultimate goal is? This is the time to be totally honest with yourself so that you can confront those obstacles and determine the steps needed to address them so that you can move on.

Exercise: Based on the information you gathered in the previous exercise, begin to plan the actions you will take to achieve your goals.

1. Schedule informational interviews with each of the people you listed as contacts beginning with your top area of interest.

2. Create a written list of questions that you will ask each person and write their responses on your form.

3. Keep your meeting brief (15-20 minutes), remembering that their time is important. You can limit your questions to no more than five, and always ask the same final question: "Who else do you know that I might speak to about this?" In doing so you're building your network.

4. Always follow up with a personal thank you within 48 hours.

5. Keep your interview information organized in folders or a binder.

6. Based on what you have learned, which companies or business opportunities should you explore? You may want to look into owning your own business, consulting,

pursuing contract work, or putting together a portfolio career that includes more than one occupation.

7. Should you choose a more traditional route, identify five companies that you think would be a good match for your skills and experience.

8. Using your network, identify one or more people who have been employed or are currently employed there that you could contact to assist you in the hiring process. If you do not know the individual personally, ask someone in your network to introduce you.

9. Begin to research the company to learn what its needs are and how you can meet those.

10. Engage in the application and interview process.

Once you have achieved your goals outlined in your strategic plan, be sure to celebrate it as a victory to your commitment. If your goal was to be employed in a technical position in a large company earning six figures, and you achieve that through your plan, put together an event to acknowledge that. You might want to include those who were on your list of resources as a way to thank them for being a part of your success.

Affirmation:

I recognize that strategic planning is the foundation for achieving my desired outcomes and I remain flexible and adaptable to changes that may arise during my job search.

Stay the course

"It's not whether you get knocked down:
it's whether you get up."
– Vince Lombardi

When you're going through a transition you will find that some days will be easier to deal with than others. Accept that there will be setbacks and disappointments as part of the natural process of reaching your ultimate destination. Your inclination may be to want to give up, asking yourself if the effort is worth it. The real question here is, "Are YOU worth it?" Whether or not you choose to proceed in spite of adversity is based on your answer to that question. Whatever feelings you are having in the moment are valid whether they be positive or negative. Those feelings can influence what you decide to do next, so recognize that they are temporary in response to your current situation. They will pass as circumstances change. What can you do to affect those changes?

This would be a good time to refer to your strategic plan. Where are you in that process and how does what is occurring affect that plan? Perhaps one of your resources has done their due diligence and a contact they thought would be vital is no longer available. Time to rethink Plan A and pursue Plan B. Who else might be a source of information for the action step you identified? It may be necessary to review your network and reach out to several of them, defining the specifics of what you need. Remember that they each maintain their own extended network. The more specific you are, the more likely they are to identify a potential contact for you.

Exercise: As you move through your strategic plan you will be gathering new information along the way. Ask yourself: What information do I need to achieve my goals? What resources do I need to call upon to provide me with this information? What do I need to do next based on what I learn, and by when do I plan to do them? Use the chart below to track this information.

New information	Resources	Next steps

In your effort to change fields, you may learn that there is a specific certification or license required. You will need to research educational resources and what is involved to apply. How are courses offered? Do you have to attend a brick and mortar campus, complete your studies online, or a combination of both? If it's a brick and mortar campus, what does that mean in terms of its location and distance from you? Would it mean having to relocate to attend their program? What would be the out-of-pocket cost to you and is there financial aid available? What are we talking about in terms of the time needed to complete such a program and how does your current age factor into this? Any or all of these questions should be considered as part of your strategic plan.

Once you take into consideration what you have learned from your situation, it's time to decide how it affects your ultimate goal. There was a point in my life when I considered going into business for myself in a new field. I had had some success with this type of work so I knew I had the basic skills for it to be a realistic option. I contacted several people who were currently employed in the field and asked them about their experience with it. While each of them shared how much satisfaction they derived from what they did, they also pointed out what would be required with the initial time and expense to go into this line of work. I weighed the advantages and disadvantages and decided that this was not a path for me. It provided a renewed sense of energy and commitment related to my current job. At the same time, I could continue to develop the skills related to the other field and apply them as part of my avocation.

When you're in transition you may notice a difference in how you experience time. Your perception of time when you're anxious or fearful can become distorted. You tend to sense that time is passing slower than what is measured on the clock. This may account for you becoming impatient and irritable while waiting for a return phone call or email. This is a common report among those who are looking for employment. When you're functioning out of a state of neediness, responses from others feel like they are taking forever. You will often hear, "I can't believe they haven't gotten back to me yet. It has been three days and I have

> *"Patience, but with a healthy sense of urgency. Staying connected to others."*
> – JC, Director, Product Management

heard nothing." This is quite different from when you're actively engaged in a task requiring you to use your skills on a specific task. The passing of a three-day period might be accompanied by, "I can't believe how quickly time has passed. It feels like I just started." The difference is the emotional state with which you view time. When you're feeling anxious about time, stop and remind yourself that this is natural for someone in transition. Then find some way to channel your anxiety into a productive task. You may want to have a list of activities to draw from that range from honing one of your job skills to cleaning out your closet.

To stay on track at this time it will be necessary to surround yourself with supportive people. There is little benefit to expending the energy needed to maintain your focus while those around you are constantly reminding you of the tolls of unemployment. "When are you going to find a job?" "You're being too picky." "Just take whatever comes along." These are words that will only increase your stress levels and most likely lead you to make a decision that you will regret later on. If you hear such questions and statements, thank the other person for their concern. Ask them if they have any particular ideas that would help your job search. Be open to what they tell you and respond that you will take their suggestions into consideration. If they cannot provide constructive suggestions, tell them that you would be open to having a conversation with them should that occur. As much as you might be tempted, there is no need to go on the offensive with them. Tap into your support system and have a discussion on how they handle such statements and how they deflect them to keep going.

One of the biggest challenges to staying the course is maintaining your optimism, especially when you're unsure as to how long the

"Ride the wave and see where it takes me."
– JH, Patent Attorney

transition is going to last. It's much easier to be optimistic when you know that the situation will be changing in less than a month. What happens when that month stretches into six months and then a year? One strategy is to refer to the journal you have been keeping on the actions you have taken on a daily basis to find employment. Review your actions and congratulate yourself on what you have been doing. If you find it difficult to acknowledge your accomplishments, invite a friend for coffee and have them do it for you. In doing so, see if there is anything else you can be doing to increase the likelihood of being hired.

Affirmation:

I remain focused on my goals concentrating on the opportunities that lie ahead rather than dwelling on past disappointments.

Key Learning Points

- Networking is a valuable way to connect with others.
- Keeping a written record can serve as a reminder of progress being made toward achieving a goal.
- Without clarity of direction, it is difficult to create a plan for reaching a destination.
- Setbacks and disappointments are a natural part of transition.

What is your story around commitment as you read through this chapter? What was it that triggered your thoughts around this?

How to support someone in transition

"Help one another; there's no time like the present and no present like the time."
– James Durst

How to support someone in transition

This chapter is dedicated to those of you who know of someone going through a transition. This can be particularly challenging when the person is unemployed over a period of time. If you're living with the person it will be nearly impossible to avoid being affected by their situation. There can be a change in income, in lifestyle, and in the emotional atmosphere of the home. No one is more acutely aware of that than the person who is out of work. It can sometimes feel like a sentence that has no chance for parole. There will be days that are fraught with tension over unpaid bills and unexpected expenses. The closer you are to the situation, the more likely you will be to experience feelings of frustration, hopelessness, anger, and depression yourself. Remember that you're also going through a transition and that you're grieving the loss of what was. This may range from having a relationship with the other person based on their position with a specific company to having to assume total responsibility for covering household expenses when your family member is unemployed.

The following sections are designed to provide suggestions for how to support the other person during this time of uncertainty. The suggestions come from the ranks of people who are in job search mode who are well aware that they are not going through this in isolation. Your level of support is based on your proximity and the amount of time you spend together. The prior five chapters contain tools and strategies that can be adapted to what you're experiencing. Refer to them as needed.

Remind them that they are not alone

"Many people need desperately to receive this message:
'I feel and think much as you do, care about many of
the things you care about, although most people do not
care about them. You are not alone.'"
– Kurt Vonnegut

When a person receives notice that they are no longer employed, there can be a tendency to withdraw from social contacts. This can be attributed to several factors. The person may feel shame, embarrassment, guilt, or hurt. Having to continually explain their circumstances to those around them only serves to fan those feelings, and they find themselves caught in a loop that focuses on the loss. They may be spending time analyzing what went wrong and how they might have prevented it from happening. They could be seeking answers from within as to how they are going to handle their financial responsibilities. There is a tendency to isolate when this occurs.

This is a time for you to share your concern over their loss, taking time to be sensitive to their feelings. Ask them if they know of anyone else who is in a similar situation. Did the company create a support network so that people could process the experience leading to a positive outcome? Are there any support groups in the area for people who are also unemployed? One resource is the Riley Guide, which can assist in directing the job seeker to a local group. If someone you know appears to be struggling with the emotional aspects of unemployment, this could be a way for them to connect with others in the same situation. It also takes the pressure off of you to have to be the sole source of support when you're going through your own issues.

> *"I was able to spend more time with the family and perform activities I wasn't able to perform while working. This transition gave me time to think about my career and what I wanted to do with my life."*
> — CR, Manager, Customer Solutions

Exercise: List three people you know who are going through a transition of some type. Write at least two actions you can take to be of support. Choose one action that you can take today to support at least one of these individuals in your life. After completing it, write how you felt doing this.

Affirmation:

I stand beside you with unwavering encouragement reminding you that your aspirations are supported by those who believe in your potential.

Name of person	Actions you can take	How you felt afterward

Demonstrate caring

*"...you'll find that being a friend is to like a person
for who they are, even the parts you don't understand. You
don't have to understand, or do the same,
or live their lives for them. If you truly care for them,
then you want them to be who they are; that was
why you liked them in the first place.*
-Terry Goodkind

Take time to ask yourself how the other person might be feeling at this moment. This may be evident through their words and body language. If their energy appears to be low, a statement as simple as, "You look like you don't seem to have much pep. Is that accurate?" If the answer is a positive, let the other person know that you're there to listen. Right now there could be questions of self-worth and self-identity. Begin by listening before attempting to intervene. Responding to concerns with "It's not so bad" or "You know, you're luckier than a lot of other people out there" will not likely help the other person feel better. Sometimes caring is best expressed by saying nothing. Sometimes it's best expressed through a smile or a hug. If you're offering a hug, take a cue from the other person and their receptiveness to it. Begin with, "You look like you could use a hug. "Are you up for that?" Then respect the response you receive.

Think of ways to express your appreciation for even the smallest things that you see in that person. Just make sure you don't overdo it. It may come across as insincere and patronizing. "Thanks for picking up the items we need for dinner tonight" or "I appreciate the time you spent helping Susie with her homework. You do such a great job of explaining things in a way that makes sense." Be specific in pointing out what you see being done. It can help to identify traits and skills that could be incorporated into a future job. You can also ask for assistance on a project that will take their mind off of their problems. The key is to find something that you can do together. It may involve helping you prepare for a children's party, changing the oil in your car, or painting a room. Keep the conversation light based on the activity, but be open to talking about what is happening with the job search if the subject comes up.

Be willing to be generous with your time while at the same time making sure that your own needs are cared for. Know that the current situation will eventually change. Remind yourself that someday the circumstances may be reversed and it's you who need to know that others care.

> *"I was able to spend more time with the family and perform activities I wasn't able to perform while working. This transition gave me time to think about my career and what I wanted to do with my life."*
> — CR, Manager, Customer Solutions

Exercise: Think of three people you know who are experiencing a transition at this time. Next to each person's name, write three traits and/or skills that you have observed in them. Now write a specific situation that you saw them demonstrate that trait or skill. Be sure to share that with the person.

Name of person	Trait or Skill Observed	Specific Situation

Affirmation:

Your dreams matter to me, and I am here to offer my support and encouragement every step of the way in achieving them.

Provide encouragement

"Go confidently in the direction of your dreams.
Live the life you have imagined."
– Henry David Thoreau

For some individuals, no longer working in the same position can be a ticket to new opportunities. What became a daily performance of routine tasks can now be replaced by a chance to move into a new arena. You may see the person exhibiting a level of excitement and enthusiasm that hasn't been observed in years. This is a time to listen as dreams are shared since they are the seeds of possibility. When you hear, "I've always wanted to be a pilot" or "My dream has always been to own a restaurant," allow the person to tell their story around it. Encourage them to explore what it would take to achieve their goal. I have worked with many clients who arrive with a dream. What they often lack is the plan, the commitment, and the support to achieve it.

Don't be afraid to ask what it would take to make their dream a reality. Ask them what the fascination is for wanting to pursue this. Most likely they have been interested in this type of work for years, sometimes since childhood. I often ask clients what they enjoyed playing and fantasizing about as children. For many of us, it's the element of play that we incorporate into our livelihoods. When this element is no longer present, work can diminish in its appeal. How often have you heard someone say, "I just don't enjoy work as much as I used to. It's lost all of its fun." Listen to how having fun in the new position plays into its attraction. If this is the case, mention it. "When you talk about doing this kind of work, I can hear the excitement in your voice, and your face lights up." That is usually an indicator of what they are passionate about.

Encourage them to think more about this new path and what would be needed to learn if it's right for them. This is where the plan begins. You may discover that the enthusiasm and drive continue or that the information they gather becomes the source for reconsideration. In speaking to those who either currently work or have worked in the new field of interest, the person may find that the work isn't as glamorous as they imagined. The hours, training, and initial pay might not match what they were expecting. If the goal is to become a doctor and the person is 50 years old, the cost and time to complete medical school may be beyond what is acceptable. Allow the person to make those decisions on his or her own. Words of encouragement do not include. "You're too old for that," "Stick with something you know," or "How could you ever afford to pay for your schooling at this time in your life?" Those are judgments likely based on how you would approach such a change. Instead ask, "How would you factor that into your plan?"

As you hear progress reports, acknowledge the time and effort that have been put into them. Ask how this information has been helpful in determining their next steps. In some cases what they learn may be cause for a change in direction. Perhaps they researched a field of interest and learned that the demand for this type of work is declining or that the skills required are beyond what they originally thought them to be. Rather than telling them that this should end their quest, ask what it was about the original idea that they found to be so attractive. If they were thinking about going into the medical field, what aspect of that appealed to them? Perhaps it was an interest in how the body works or supporting people in maintaining their health. What are other occupations they could consider that include these interests and could be pursued with training and experience closer to their current level of expertise?

Remind the person you know that gathering such information takes time. There may be a rush to act on what they know, and there may be a critical piece missing. Encourage them to continue to learn about their area of interest so that they can make an informed decision. If they are considering opening their own business, it would be beneficial to know that most of these ventures do not succeed because of lack of information, skills, and the capital to cover expenses. Encourage them to speak to those who have at least five years as successful business owners to identify the challenges they faced and how they dealt with them.

When you're unsure as to what you can do to encourage another, simply ask, "How can I help you at this time?" Then listen to their response. If they tell you that they don't know, you can ask probing questions as to where they are now. This can include asking about how they are feeling about their job search or if there is something that seems to be blocking their forward momentum. Give them the time they need to respond as a way of being respectful of their process. "I'll check in with you in a day or two if I don't hear from you," is a way of letting them know that you care about their wellbeing. Once you make that commitment, be sure to follow up as promised.

> *"I felt frustrated, pulled down by my loved ones,*
> *and not offering any support made me feel discouraged,*
> *drained, and led to a lack of motivation unless I picked*
> *[up] my bags and travelled to another planet to start*
> *things over again. But I know that's not possible because*
> *I'd miss my kids. So I'm battling low morale [and a] sense*
> *of overwhelming to find a new career and a*
> *renewed spirit and goals and motivation."*
> – RB

Exercise: Think about a person you know who may be feeling confused about what direction to take in their life. One way to support the person is by asking the following questions.

1. What would you be doing that would create enthusiasm and excitement for you?
2. What it would take to achieve that?
3. To whom could you speak who does or has done this type of work?
4. How could you contact this person?

5. What questions would you ask them?
6. If you learned that this was something you were interested in pursuing, what would your next steps be?
7. How committed would you be to pursuing your dream?
8. What do you think might become an obstacle and how could you overcome it?
9. How can I support you in this process?

Affirmation:

I offer genuine praise and recognition for your efforts, celebrating your strengths, achievements, and resilience.

Use active listening

"Listening is such a simple act. It requires us to be present, and that takes practice, but we don't have to do anything else. We don't have to advise, or coach, or sound wise. We just have to be willing to sit there and listen."
– Margaret J. Wheatley

When you're engaged in active listening you are reflecting back your understanding of what the speaker has just shared with you. It requires that you give the speaker your undivided attention so that you capture both their verbal and nonverbal communication. We know that only about 7% of what a person communicates is with their actual words. The majority of the message rests with their affect, their tone of voice, their facial expressions, and their posture. To truly listen it's necessary that you suspend your judgments and reactions to the message as it is being presented to you. This is not always easy to do because of our tendency to want to mentally prepare our response. In doing so we may miss the essence of what the other person is trying to communicate.

One technique for active listening is what is referred to as *paraphrasing*. This involves restating the speaker's words without attaching intent or agreement. After you paraphrase the statement, you seek acknowledgment from the speaker as to your accuracy. You're looking for a "Yes" or "No" response. If you receive a "No, that's not what I am saying," then request that the person restate it. Perhaps there was too much information to retain and having it broken down into shorter sound bites would help in your understanding of it. You can preface your paraphrasing with, "Let me see if I understand this correctly" or "Let me make sure I am hearing you" or "I want to be clear on what you're saying." This sets the tone for what you heard them say. If overused during a conversation, this technique can be somewhat annoying to the speaker who may blurt out, "I just said that!"

One important way to differentiate between thoughts and feelings being expressed is in the use of the word "like" in a statement. "I feel **like** you're not listening to me" or "I feel **like** you don't really care about what is best for me," are actually thoughts, not feelings. The person is stating that they don't **think** you're listening to them or that they do not **think** you have their best interest at heart. When you hear such statements, rephrase them with feeling statements such as, "So you're feeling ignored" or "You're feeling uncared for." Then allow them to respond. This removes the likelihood that you will move into taking a defensive stance with their statement.

Another technique involves asking probing questions for clarification. This occurs when you're uncertain about what the person is attempting to communicate and you need more information. These questions traditionally start with "What, Who, When, Why, Where, and How." "**What** were you feeling when you were told that you were being laid off tomorrow?" "**Who** was present when this information was shared with you?" "**When** did you first have a sense that a layoff would occur?" "**Why** do you think your position was included in the layoff?" "**Where** do you think your work duties were transferred?" "**How** are you feeling right now about this situation?" Allow the person time to think about the response before answering, as they may not be able to access that information immediately. Accept "I don't know. I'll have to think about that and get back to you," without probing further on that topic. You may find that, as a result of a probing question, the conversation may proceed in an entirely different direction.

A third technique is referred to as *mirroring*. This technique is used when a person begins a conversation with a feeling such as, "I'm really upset right now" or "I can't believe what you just did." To respond effectively you need to know what the underlying situation is. Begin with statements such as "You sound...", "You look ...", or "You seem..." followed by your best estimate of their emotional state based on their words and body language.

If the other person tells you that you are incorrect in your assessment, don't go on the defense. If you continue to try to guess, it may add to the frustration of the other person moving through the problem. Ask them what would be a closer description of what they are experiencing. If you give feedback that the person looks angry and they negate that assessment, you could ask if there was a word that more accurately described the situation.

Mirroring can also occur at the nonverbal level. It involves reflecting back facial expressions and physical gestures. The speaker smiles or frowns and you smile or frown back. If the speaker leans forward, you do the same. If the speaker raises or lowers his voice level, you correspond. This is done to establish a connection with one another. Be aware that if you do this in a tense or stressful situation, it can escalate the problem. If you encounter someone who is in the throes of anger, raising your voice in intensity to match theirs may only make matters worse. Be conscious of what you're dealing with and choose a method of responding most appropriate to the situation.

The goal of using the mirroring technique is to gather the facts related to the expressed emotions. You can learn what is underlying the feelings and help the person identify what they need to address as to what is going on with them. Using this technique helps to strengthen your relationship by providing a sense of understanding and acceptance. Once you both are clearer on the issue at hand, you can move forward with identifying the steps that can be taken to alleviate the situation.

Active listening requires you to give your full attention to the speaker. If you're unable to do so, share that immediately. "It's really important that I give you my full attention and right now my focus is on something else." Then negotiate a time in the near future when you can be completely available to them. Given the seriousness of what the other person is experiencing, it may be necessary for you to stop what you're doing and focus on their needs. Remember that there may be a perceived difference in what that severity would look like. A response such as, "You mean you interrupted what I was doing for something as minor as that," could be perceived as hurtful or insensitive. Let the other person know that you're totally present by facing them directly and making eye contact. If you're on the telephone, end your conversation to avoid distractions and interruptions. Turn off the television, computer, or radio. If you have others present such as children, request that they give you the time needed for a private conversation.

Allow for silences and pauses while you're listening. We typically allow about three seconds before a response is expected; sometimes it may need to be significantly longer. This permits the speaker to formulate their thoughts and verbalize them in a way that makes sense. It may be a challenge to sit or stand silently next to the person without starting a conversation in your head. This may take some practice on your part, and it's necessary to sustain your attention.

All active listening requires a conscious attending to not only what the person is saying, but also how you're choosing to respond to what you hear. Vary the techniques you use when listening to another share what they are going through at the moment. Be mindful of the words and body language and what you will say in response to them. The role of listener is a powerful one in helping someone who may be experiencing disappointment, frustration, or anger.

Exercise: On the following page, choose one of the three techniques contained in this section. Make a decision to consciously practice the technique during the upcoming week. Use the chart to monitor your success with the technique.

Speaker and issue	My response	What worked	Improvement

Affirmation:

I give my undivided attention to you, allowing you to express your thoughts, feelings, and aspirations without interruption.

Reciprocate

> *"There are many benefits to this process of listening.*
> *The first is that good listeners are created as people feel*
> *listened to. Listening is a reciprocal process—we become*
> *more attentive to others if they have attended to us."*
> – Margaret J. Wheatley

There are a number of ways to approach reciprocity. One way is through active listening techniques as described in the previous section. As you engage in being actively involved in the listening process, ask yourself what you perceive to be the benefits of doing so. Are you demonstrating care and respect for the other person? Are you strengthening the bond between you? Are you practicing empathy? Is this what you would hope for when you're in need of someone to talk to you about a specific situation? In this case, it's a matter of getting what you give. If you come across as a person who is unwilling to give attention to another, it can affect another's willingness to be there for you. If your response to this is, "I don't have time to listen to other people's problems. They need to figure it out for themselves," it may be affecting your connection to others. Listening skills can be learned and strengthened through practice.

Reciprocity also consists of returning one good deed with another. It takes you out of the realm of "What's in it for me?' and replaces it with, "How can I be of help to you at this time?" There is a famous story of two groups of people who are now in the afterlife. In their current existence, they have arms that are several feet in length. In front of each group is a banquet table filled with all the delectable foods they can eat. The one group is starving because their arms are too long to get the food from the table to their mouths. The other group is thriving because they are feeding each other. Which group would you prefer to be a part of? As you find yourself in the presence of those who are going through a transition, consider how you can be of support.

When meeting with other professionals during networking events, it's standard practice to share names of individuals and companies who might be interested in their services. This element of reciprocity increases the pool of potential clients. If you're seen as a resource for such contacts, people will welcome your presence. The same is true for the job seeker. If you know of an opportunity or a contact that might be helpful, freely offer the information. The reverse often happens when you adopt this approach. Think of the effect that "Let me introduce you to my friend who works at Company X" or "I'll be happy to put you in touch with my cousin who is knowledgeable about what is happening in that industry" has on building a sense of hope and anticipation. What a difference it would make if everyone was committed to the success of others.

Exercise: Write the names of five people you know who might be going through a transition of some type in their life. Next to each person's name, write a list of ways that you might offer assistance and support. Choose one or more of those ways the next opportunity you have to interact with that person. How did that work out?

Person	Possible ways to be of assistance	How that worked

Affirmation:

I embrace the power of reciprocity, trusting that my support will be reciprocated in unexpected and meaningful ways.

Return calls and emails

> *"Not returning phone calls is the severest form*
> *of torture in the civilized world."*
> – Marisha Pessl

Have you ever had someone tell you that they would be contacting you in a given span of time and you wait and wait and wait for the call or email? You arrange your schedule so that you're available and nothing happens. Now imagine what that is like for a person who is depending on that contact to determine the next steps in their job search. I experienced the feelings related to that when an HR representative assured me that I would be hearing from him before the end of the day. I planned accordingly and waited. It wasn't until almost 24 hours later that I received the call with no apologies or explanation as to why he had not followed up as promised. This sends a strong message of their customer relations' policy and how they view people. Needless to say, that deeply colored my opinion of their organization.

When you're in a position where a response is requested, consider the other person. This is a situation that calls for empathy on your part. It's understandable that we all have busy schedules. There are several approaches to take when returning calls and emails that demonstrate respect for the other person and will elevate their opinion of you. When I was a school administrator I kept a phone log that included the name of the caller, the time of the call, and a brief description of the message and action needed to be taken. I then assigned a priority to the call. If it was coded as a "1," I returned the call immediately. In some cases, the call could be returned up to 24 hours later making it a "2." Those that could be returned within the next few days were indicated as a "3." I marked off each call as I completed it along with any additional actions needed. That may have included a call back with a status report.

A second approach was to respond with a message that I had received their call but was not able to provide an answer within a given time period. Then I would inform them of when they could expect to hear from me within a reasonable amount of time. This is what is referred to as "professional courtesy." From my conversations with people, I know it has become a rare practice. You're acknowledging your unavailability while at the same time assuring them that you're aware of their needs. It helps reduce everyone's stress levels.

If you have the luxury of having an assistant who can access your business calls, he or she can respond directly to those who require a simple answer or inform the person that you will be getting back to them personally within a certain time. One statement I caution people on using is "Mr. Smith is very busy right now. He'll get back to you sometime later." I tell people that this can be interpreted as "Mr. Smith has priorities and you are not one of them." Think about the times in which you have received a prompt response and the times that you were uncertain when you would hear back and how you felt in each situation. I usually begin the return call with an expression of gratitude when I hear back in a timely manner.

If you're the recipient of a call on a more personal level, it's just as important to respond as soon as possible. Even if you do not have time to talk, a simple, "I received your call and will get back to you later today to give you the time we need to talk. What time works best for you?" is all that is required. That takes about 10 seconds of your time.

Exercise: In the following chart, track your commitments to return calls and emails in a timely manner to those in need of your support. Code your responses as

1. (Immediate attention),
2. (within the next 24 hours),
3. (within the next 72 hours).

In the third column, write the date of completion.

Person	Code (1,2,3)	Date of Completion

Affirmation:

I listen actively to the messages left for me, honoring deadlines and expectations while demonstrating genuine interest and engagement.

Offer to help

*"Give more, so that we can build more, put
interest in understanding another more in whatever
actions one might carry out in life. Because we all
are fighting for survival against adversaries and are
sometimes falling, but if we stand together and help shield
and strengthen one another, imagine the world
that we will live in together, having more happiness
with one another, at one another's side."*
– Jonathan Anthony Burkett

As social beings, it's in our nature to help one another. When you observe someone struggling or in pain, offer your support in whatever way is needed. In most cases, you will find that the mere fact that you're present lessens their feelings of isolation and helplessness. People often are reluctant to help because they don't know what that would look like. The simple solution to that is to ask, "What do you need right now to get through this?" You may be able to provide for that need directly or suggest a resource. When you respond with only, "I can't help you," it only adds to the sense of desperation and hopelessness that the other person is feeling. Spend time listening and responding to concerns as a way to show you care.

Think of ways that you can be of service to those in need. It may be by teaching someone to learn a new skill. If someone is having a problem with using the computer, begin by asking them what they are trying to accomplish. Perhaps they don't understand how to create a file or how to put together a slide presentation with graphics. Then gently take them through the learning process by inquiring on how they learn best. Are they a visual, auditory, or tactile learner? I personally learn best by observing someone and writing down the steps to complete a task. Then I follow what I have written down to see if I can do it independently while they watch me. Once I am successful with that, I am on my way. Take time to find out what works best for the other person and teach them within that framework.

Think of ways to connect people. You typically do this when you hear someone ask if you know of a plumber or the best person for a haircut. You're connecting and referring all the time. Ask yourself how difficult it is to engage in this practice. When you listen to someone and what they are seeking, file that information away for future reference. The more specific the request, the easier it will be to identify a resource. When someone is in job search mode, the words that can show that you're there for them can be, "Let me introduce you to Joe, who works in that field" or "Would you like me to have Mary, who works in this industry, look over your resume with a fresh set of eyes and get her thoughts on its effectiveness?" You probably know more people than you think, and helping someone with a particular need creates a filter that you use when speaking to others who might be of assistance.

Send messages letting the other person know that you're thinking about them. The note you send may be just what is needed to lift the spirits of someone who may not feel encouraged that day. The message does not need to be lengthy. It can also include an invitation to either have them call you or you telling them of your plan to call. Make sure you're specific in when you plan to reach out to them and commit to taking that action. You don't want to reinforce what they may already be thinking about people not caring. Be ready to use your active listening skills outlined in the beginning of the chapter.

While it's important to offer your help at this time, remember to be respectful of the other person's wishes should they express a need to be alone for the time being. Some people need time to process new information or to deal with an unexpected change of events. If the person asks to be left alone, you can ask if they mind you checking in with them and establish a date that you will do that. If you can't get a firm commitment on that, consider sending a card or an email reminding them that you're there for them.

If you see someone who is experiencing a deep depression or anger over their situation, you may need to intervene. If you hear the person describing the desperation related to their job loss, it should not be taken lightly. Find out if there is a plan for moving forward positively in their job search. If you're told that it's hopeless and there is no way out of their dilemma, it may be necessary to contact someone who can assess the situation better than you. I have sat with friends in this position and was ready to call 911 if need be. In one case I learned that the only thing my friend needed was to have someone show that they were there to listen without judging. The 911 call never happened, but I was ready to take that action as part of our friendship.

Exercise: In Column A list the names of people you know who are in transition. In Column B write the type of support they need such as contacts within a specific company or industry. In Column C list your resources that could benefit the person. After talking to the person who is seeking support, create a plan for how the support or information will be provided (Column D).

Person	Support Needed	Resources	Follow up Plan

Affirmation:

I genuinely offer my expertise, insights, and resources to those in need, offering encouragement and belief in their abilities.

Key Learning Points

- Simply being there for another is a valuable source of support during transition.
- Encouragement, rather than judgment, leads to exploration of new possibilities.
- Active listening promotes clarification and understanding.
- Helping others becomes its own reward.
- Returning messages is a sign of respect.

What is your story around helping others who are experiencing a transition as you read through this chapter? What was it that triggered your thoughts around this?

The next steps

"If I am what I have, and if I lose what I have,
then who am I?"
– Erich Fromm

Changes in life are inevitable. You may be going through a divorce, relocating to another city or state, dealing with a significant health issue, or losing your job. Whatever had been the previous condition is no more. You're now single, your familiar surroundings and network of friends will now shift, you can no longer participate in your favorite pastimes, or the doors to your workplace have closed. Now what? The questions become, "How long will I be single before I meet someone to love?" "What will the place I move to be like and who will I meet as new friends?" "Will I ever be able to hike through mountain trails or run a marathon?" "How long will I be out of work and what will I do to survive until I find a new job?" With these questions comes a flood of emotions that can overwhelm you to where you wonder what it will take to just make it through the day. Your identity is shaken to the core based on what is no longer there. Who and what will emerge as time passes?

It is at this time that it's important to recall those events from your past that required a change in your life and what you did to reach a new beginning. Were you the type of person who focused on the moment and what you could do to feel like you were in control? Did you tap into strategies that worked for you in the past and apply them to your current situation? Did you use this time to explore possibilities? Did you employ introspection to identify what was really important to you? Did you create a logical plan for what you would do during this uncertain time? Did you seek to create a way to make sense of what was happening in your life? Did you look outside yourself to help those that you saw as having greater needs? Did you use this time to connect with friends and family to support you through the process?

Your will to survive the change before you is supported by the ways in which you cope with transition. The previous chapters are designed to provide you with tools for navigating through the uncharted territory that exists between an ending and a new beginning. There may be times when you're going through multiple changes, each with their own challenges and emotions. A loss of employment can be accompanied by a significant decrease in your bank account and an impact on your recreational activities. Your annual trips abroad are suspended until further notice and all you can afford right now is a drive to the local park. You may be feeling depressed about your job loss, frustrated with the loss of savings, and angry about not being able to visit a vacation spot you had dreamed about for years. You may move through one set of emotions more quickly than another. There is no predicting how much time it will take to work through whatever stage you are in.

Transition can be multidirectional. You may also ping-pong between feeling up one day and down the next. When I left my field of 34 years I did so feeling hopeful and excited about my future. I have learned that it's not unusual to experience feelings of euphoria as you enter into a transition. The situation I was leaving no longer provided the satisfaction I felt when I was the peak of my career there. I was sure that something better would appear soon. As the weeks and months passed without a job offer, those feelings were replaced by disappointment and discouragement. During this time I joined a professional networking group and began to feel hopeful again. I felt like I was bouncing all over the emotional spectrum. Working through a transition may not always follow a linear path before coming out the other side.

Avoid approaching the process as a predictable set of steps based on the books you have read. At any time along the way you may experience a set of circumstances that you hadn't anticipated. You could be caught up in the anger today around how you were let go from your last position and receive an unexpected offer tomorrow for your dream job. Would you turn it down because you hadn't worked through the other stages of loss? Sometimes the process of grieving a loss can be short-circuited by new information. *Just be open to it.*

Remember that transition is also multidimensional. While you may be experiencing a variety of changes in your life, those changes are having a direct and an indirect effect on those around you. Your job loss will most definitely affect the lives of family members. Your spouse will have to rethink a daily routine and how expenses will now be covered. There may be anger and resentment over a change in lifestyle when it's necessary to cut back on the activities that the income from your job would have covered. Your children may need to participate in the austerity measures that follow a long period of unemployment. That will certainly generate emotions on their part. Extended family and friends will have their own thoughts about your situation and may be all too willing to share those thoughts with you. It will be important to recognize this when those uninvited thoughts and feelings are communicated to you. Be ready to use your own active listening skills when this occurs. No one goes through a transition in a vacuum.

Transitions are not time-limited. I have heard people say that they are only going to dedicate a specific amount of time to a loss and then they are going to move on. We live in a society that imposes such practices. Within my employment settings you could take one day off to attend the funeral of a friend, three days for a local relative, and five days for a relative who died far enough away that it required travel time. It didn't matter how close they were to you in your attachment to them. When you returned to work you were expected to assume a "business as usual" attitude. You likely have heard, "Haven't you gotten over that yet?" when it comes to a loss in your life. That is true of losing a job, but more often comes in the form of, "When are you going to go back to work?" If you have prepared a positive response to this question, it could lead to a more productive outcome.

One of the benefits of successfully navigating through a change is that you can develop a greater awareness of your strengths. Think back to how you used your self-confidence, perseverance, acceptance, resilience, and commitment in the process. If you were to repeat the assessments in each of these areas today, how would your responses compare to your initial ones? This is evidence of the progress you have made in your journey from an ending to a new beginning. If there were any areas that you identified that you would like to continue to develop, how would you use the information related to them to create a plan for growth? Perhaps you will have a greater understanding of the value of networking or setting personal and professional goals.

The mere idea of writing this book sparked a set of strategies that I have incorporated into my own life as well as sharing them with my clients as they move through their own transitions. Completing the book allowed me to see the fallacies of the beliefs I held for years that I was incapable of writing. The process of writing has been a transition in and of itself. It began as an ending of a belief of my lack of writing abilities, then a period of disciplined writing and editing, and finally as a new beginning with a published book. Now is the time to revisit your belief system and create a plan for challenging those beliefs that no longer serve you. Then commit to following through on that plan using your internal and external resources. Take pride in your accomplishments reminding yourself of the effort and courage it took to achieve them.

You may not think that you have control over external events, and most likely that is the truth. There will always be changes in health, relationships, residence, and employment. We all eventually die, watch those close to us leave, move from one address to another, and retire from the work we do. These are the realities of life. What you can control is how you deal with these changes. It may not lessen the angst you feel while you're in the midst of change, but it can help you move through it more quickly and positively. It can help to avoid adopting a victim mentality that keeps you stuck in the anger and depression.

If you're connected to someone going through a transition, remember that it's important to acknowledge your own responses and reactions to what is happening around you. They have their own validity and require that you do what is necessary for your own well-being. Make sure that you're clear in what you can and cannot do to support others. At the same time be willing to reach out to others for support.

Be kind and gentle with yourself during these times. Be open to possibilities that may come from the most unexpected sources. Remember that you're not alone. Isolation is self-imposed. Reach out to others even when you don't want to. That is probably when you need it the most. Deal with what is in front of you and consciously plan to address it. When your new beginning appears, you will have a greater sense of stability and a stronger sense of self. Enjoy it while it lasts, as another transition awaits you as part of the human condition. The more aware you are of the process, the more prepared you will be to weather it.

The 30-Day Job Seeker Challenge

Building Self-Confidence, Commitment,
Acceptance,Resilience, and Perseverance

Day 1: **Confidence Boost** List five accomplishments or positive experiences from your personal and professional journey. Reflect on these moments as a way to boost your self-confidence. Carry this self-assuredness into your job search interactions and interviews.

Day 2: **Building Support Systems** Identify individuals in your life who can provide emotional support during your job search. Share your progress and ask for advice when needed. Remember, you don't have to navigate this journey alone.

Day 3: **Facing Rejection** Think of rejection as redirection and an opportunity for growth. Take note of the lessons learned from each rejection and use them to improve your approach. Stay resilient and persist in pursuing new opportunities.

Day 4: **Cultivating Resilience** Identify one obstacle or challenge you've encountered in your job search. Consider different strategies and resources to overcome it. Practice resilience by adapting to setbacks and maintaining a positive mindset.

Day 5: **Strengthening Networking Skills** Attend a networking event either virtually or in-person. Practice your active listening skills, ask engaging questions, and genuinely connect with others. Expand your network and capitalize on opportunities to showcase your skills and knowledge.

Day 6: **Self-Reflection** Set aside time to reflect on your strengths, accomplishments, and unique qualities. Write down three things you appreciate about yourself and set an intention to carry this self-confidence throughout the challenge.

Day 7: **Elevator Pitch** Craft a compelling elevator pitch that effectively communicates your unique skills, experiences, and career goals. Be sure to include your brand statement. Use your pitch as a tool to make a strong impression in networking or interview situations.

Day 8: **Embracing Acceptance** Know that rejection and setbacks are part of the job search process. Remember that each NO leads the ultimate YES. Practice self-acceptance by reframing failures as opportunities for growth and learning. Remind yourself of your self-worth and resilience by using affirmations.

Day 9: **Resilient Mindset** When facing a challenge or setback, reframe negative thoughts into positive ones by focusing on solutions, growth, and the lessons learned. Maintain an optimistic perspective to strengthen your resilience.

Day 10: **Setting Clear Goals** Define your short-term and long-term career goals. Then create a specific action plan with measurable objectives that align with these goals. Commit to pursuing these goals with determination.

Day 11: **Continuous Learning** Expand your knowledge and skills in your desired field by taking a course, attending a webinar, or reading a relevant book. Embrace lifelong learning and apply new insights to enhance your job search strategy.

Day 12: **Building Professional Presence** Review and update your online professional profiles on a regular basis. Ensure they accurately reflect your skills, experiences, and career goals to attract potential employers.

Day 13: **Learning from Setbacks** Reflect on a recent setback and identify the lessons learned. Ask how you can improve your approach as you move forward. Apply these insights to refine your job search strategy and increase your chances of success.

Day 14: **Strengthening Resilience through Self-Care** Practice self-care activities that rejuvenate your mind and body. Engage in exercise, hobbies, or activities that bring you joy. By doing so, you enhance resilience and boost overall confidence.

Day 15: **Networking Power** Reach out to at least two individuals in your professional network. Share your goals and offer support to others. This will serve to strengthen your connections and expand your network to create new opportunities.

Day 16: **Embracing Flexibility** Incorporate flexibility into your job search strategy. Use this time to explore new industries, roles, or approaches that align with your skills and interests. Consider the possibilities that emerge while being open to new opportunities.

Day 17: **Accepting Feedback** Welcome feedback and constructive criticism from trusted mentors, peers, and professionals in your field as an opportunity for growth. Use the feedback received to refine your skills and enhance your desirability as a potential candidate for a position.

Day 18: **Self-Reflection and Adjustment** Reflect on your progress throughout the challenge. List the strategies that have been effective and identify areas that may require adjustment. Use this information to adapt your approach to maximize your chances of success.

Day 19: **Celebrating Milestones** Reflect on your achievements and progress so far, no matter how small. Celebrate each milestone reached during your job search journey. Plan to reward yourself along the way and acknowledge the progress you've made towards your goals.

Day 20: **Mindfulness Practice** Engage in a mindfulness activity, such as meditation or deep breathing exercises. As you engage in this activity, be mindful of your thoughts and emotions, allowing yourself to be present in each moment. This practice augments clarity and focus.

Day 21: **Gratitude Practice** List three things you are grateful for today in your job search journey. Express gratitude directly to those who have supported and encouraged you. Expressing gratitude enhances positivity and resilience throughout the process.

Day 22: **Collaboration and Support** Offer support and assistance to others in their job search journey. Share resources, provide feedback, or make introductions within your network as way to reciprocate the support you have received from others.

Day 23: **Dealing With Stress** Make note of any sources of stress in your life today. Ask yourself what you can do to reduce their effect. Focus on what you can control as a way to reduce it.

Day 24: **Recharging Day** Take a day to relax, reenergize, and engage in activities that bring you joy and pleasure. By doing so, you recharge your energy to approach the final days of the challenge with renewed focus and determination.

Day 25: **Accountability Partner** Find an accountability partner who shares similar career goals. Schedule weekly check-ins to discuss progress, challenges, and provide mutual support. This relationship will keep you motivated and responsible for the actions you take during your job search.

Day 26: **Overcoming Self-Doubt** Challenge self-doubt by focusing on past successes and positive feedback. Remind yourself of your capabilities and strengths. Replace self-limiting beliefs with empowering affirmations that reinforce your self-confidence.

Day 27: **Persistence Pays Off** Set a daily goal to apply for a specific number of jobs or reach out to potential employers. Keep pushing forward, even in the face of obstacles. Acknowledge your efforts accepting them as your commitment to your success

Day 28: **Seek Emotional Support** Make a list of three people you know who can offer emotional support as you proceed in your job search. Reach out to each of them during the next week based on what you need at that time.

Day 29: **Regain Your Feeling of Control** Take time to reflect on what it is that you truly want in life. Reflect on your goals and values and plan for your future based on their importance in your life today.

Day 30: **Celebration and Moving Forward** Celebrate the completion of the 30-Day Job Seeker Challenge. Acknowledge your growth, commitment, and resilience. Take a moment to appreciate your journey, and move forward with confidence and optimism in pursuit of your career goals.

Appendix - Skills

Communication: How you express your thoughts and ideas

Speaking effectively

Writing concisely

Listening attentively

Expressing ideas through movement

Facilitating group discussion

Providing appropriate feedback

Negotiating

Perceiving nonverbal messages

Persuading

Reporting information

Describing feelings

Interviewing

Editing

Initiating

Comprehending written material

Research and Planning: How you gather specific knowledge and your ability to develop ways to meet future needs

Forecasting, predicting

Creating ideas

Identifying problems

Imagining alternatives

Identifying resources

Gathering information

Solving problems

Setting goals

Extracting important information

Defining needs

Analyzing

Developing evaluation strategies

Designing

Evaluating

Planning

Structuring

Synthesizing

Human Relations: How you use interpersonal skills for resolving conflict, relating to, and helping people

Developing rapport

Being sensitive

Listening

Conveying feelings

Providing support for others

Motivating

Sharing credit

Counseling

Cooperating

Delegating with respect

Representing others

Perceiving feelings, situations

Asserting

Conflict resolution

Crisis management

Helping

Nurturing

Performing

Pleasing

Organization, Management and Leadership: How your supervise, direct and guide individuals and groups in the completion of tasks

Initiating new ideas

Handling details

Coordinating tasks

Managing groups

Delegating responsibility

Teaching

Coaching

Counseling

Promoting change

Selling ideas or products

Decision making with others

Managing conflict

Supervising

Physical and Mechanical: How you use your physical abilities to manipulate tools

Accuracy

Adjusting

Assembling

Endurance

Finger dexterity

Manual dexterity

Operating

Physical coordination

Responding quickly

Physical strength

Measuring

Creative and Artistic: How you express yourself through imagination and movement

Aesthetic judgment

Dancing

Color discrimination

Depth perception

Shape discrimination

Sound discrimination

Music composition

Painting

Singing

Playing a musical instrument

Detail: How you focus on the parts that make up the whole

Attention to detail

Categorizing

Caution

Following directions

Precision

Record keeping

Thoroughness

Verifying

Work Performance: How you promote effective production and work satisfaction

Accepting instruction

Implementing decisions

Cooperating

Enforcing policies

Being punctual

Managing time

Attending to detail

Meeting goals

Enlisting help

Accepting responsibility

Setting and meeting deadlines

Organizing

Making decisions

Conforming

Dependability

Performing under pressure

Risk-taking

Self-control

Performing repetitive tasks

Flexibility

Working under adversity

About the Author

Upon completion of a master's degree in special education, David Petrovay spent more than 30 years working as a teacher, a career counselor, and a school administrator in residential schools for the blind across the country. In 1990 he was named Worker of the Year in his field in the state of Arizona. His interest in career development motivated him to pursue a PhD from the University of Arizona in Tucson, Arizona, graduating in 2008. His doctoral dissertation focused on the characteristics of individuals who chose to become teachers of the blind and visually impaired with implications for recruitment and retention of those working within this field.

Having continuously worked as an educator in a specific setting posed a challenge when he made the decision to retire from that line of employment, yet continue to work. The plan to enter a new field meant leaving the security and success of the known and entering into uncharted territory. His personal experience with the process of transition over the next year provided insights into the challenges of a job search.

Dr. Petrovay has worked in the field of career counseling and coaching for 20 years in a number of settings that include schools, nonprofits, adult career centers, and private practice. During this time he has presented on career-related topics to universities, community organizations, and employment centers. He also serves as a regular guest on KFAX radio, San Francisco, California, speaking about the state of employment on a national level as well as how to approach a job search in today's world. Dr. Petrovay is a member of the Career One Stop national advisory board that reports to the Department of Labor. He has also served on the National Advisory Council for the College of Education at the University of Arizona.

You may contact Dr. Petrovay through his email at davidpetrovay@gmail.com or by phone at (650) 400-7461. For additional information, visit his website at davidpetrovaycoaching.com

www.ingramcontent.com/pod-product-compliance
Lightning Source LLC
Chambersburg PA
CBHW071729150726
47998CB00005B/1559